I0035124

# THE
# OTHER SIDE
## OF THE TABLE

### STRATEGIC SOURCING FROM A
### SALES EXECUTIVE'S POINT OF VIEW

# THE
# OTHER SIDE
## OF THE TABLE

## STRATEGIC SOURCING FROM A
## SALES EXECUTIVE'S POINT OF VIEW

### TODD A. LEONARD

© 2016 by Todd A. Leonard All rights reserved.

All rights reserved. No part of this book may be used or reproduced in any manner whatsoever without prior written consent of the author, except as provided by the United States of America copyright law.

ISBN: 978-0-9976842-0-9

Library of Congress Control Number: 2016909153

# DEDICATION

*To my wife, Marisa, who for more than 30 years has supported me and my passion for selling that takes me on the road and away from home many weeks each year. And, to my daughter Jennifer and son Alex, who both believe I enjoy my job way too much for it to be considered work.*

# ACKNOWLEDGEMENTS

There are many more individuals than I can possibly name who have had a hand in helping and encouraging me along the way with this book. But, there are a few that bubble up to the top worth thanking here.

To Courtney Allen, one of my longest and closest friends, as well as my colleague for many years at Standard Register. He was by my side for many of the stories in the book – and offered the right suggestions as to what to change in the writing.

To Jeff Teal, the best business development executive I know. There is no one more positive or optimistic than Jeff. And, much like Courtney, Jeff was with me for many of the experiences shared in the book.

To Joe Morgan, former CEO of Standard Register. I find myself sometimes judging folks by how good they are on a sales call. And, as CEO, there was no better executive to have on sales calls than Joe. I dragged him with me to a lot of customer visits – most of which ended successfully for us. Several of the stories you will see in the book included Joe.

To Nicole Gebhardt who coached me on how to make the book marketable and enjoyable for every reader. To Crystal Yeagy who managed the project from a rough draft through the book being published. And, to my editor, Maggie Petrovic who pored over every word, sentence and paragraph ensuring the text was the best it could be without losing my message.

Throughout the book there are a number of stories I use to bring emphasis to various approaches and points. All of them are true – and personal to me in my sales career. If you think one or more of the stories is about you, whether intentional or not, it probably is. In those instances, thank you.

# FOREWORD

In today's rapidly changing business world, strategic sourcing has never been more important for companies, or more challenging. Needs are increasingly complex. Sourcing has become a critical part of overall business strategies. The required subject matter expertise is significantly different than it was just three or five years ago. And, the reliance of external solution providers, or partners, is essential to most companies' business models.

Structure within the sourcing and selling process is also very important. It must be maintained in some form, or risk is dramatically increased for the point people – but even more substantially for the enterprises themselves. A poor decision damages everyone involved, which makes process discipline critical.

I was sitting in my office one afternoon talking with Todd, when he asked me a question I wasn't prepared for, "Will you write the foreword to *The Other Side of the Table?*" He often asked me questions about strategy or positioning in a selling situation. However, this was a very different request; one far more personal. What followed was a period of reflection, partially about the topic of the book but, honestly, more about the author, Todd Leonard, and his professional journey. After 15 years of working together in a wide range of customer situations, describing Todd came easily for me – he is analytical, competent and consistent. Todd routinely reduces a complicated situation down to the important factors in a sourcing situation with ease. He confidently guides the customer toward the desired outcome, even in situations where they might have started with different viewpoints. Knowledge gathered from a broad range of engagements enhances the positioning of his response to the next opportunity.

Todd captures the emotions of the strategic sourcing process, while providing real insights surrounding the value (or lack thereof) with traditional approaches to solving business needs. How do you find the optimal pool of potential partners to help you solve complex needs? How do you narrow that to the best solution provider? Are RFPs serving the desired purpose? How much of a role does culture of the provider and sourcing team play? Who should be engaged in the sourcing process – and when? As a potential provider, when is removing yourself from a selling situation the right thing to do? Todd provides answers to these questions, and more. And, he details a disciplined approach to effectively sourcing any strategic need. But, he still leaves ample room for contemplation, showing clearly that there isn't just one way.

While working with Todd, I saw the transition of the sales process go from product to solution, relationship-based to C-level executives, procurement driven to supply chain owned and from silos where sales professionals sought control, to collaborative team selling. And, I watched him work with sourcing executives and their teams to deliver successful experiences through a proven process. Throughout the various stages, a theme of adaptability to maintain relevance evolved, which is captured in this book.

The stories shared are based on Todd's personal experience during many years of complex selling situations often resulting in wins for his company, but also some disappointments when outmaneuvered or misaligned. Honest balance, along with the subtle references within his stories, demonstrates his own personal development, while yielding great outcomes for his company and customers.

My experience in the sourcing and selling process is derived from sitting on both sides of the table – in roles ranging from product engineer to CEO, working for start-ups to a 100-year-old publicly traded company in transformation. The insights provided by Todd in *"The Other Side of the Table"* are enlightening and actionable, showing how the best deals get done so that both sides win.

**– Joe Morgan**
Founder, siY, LLC

# CONTENTS

Introduction................................................................1

**Chapter 1:** Buyer vs. Strategic Sourcing Executive.................5

**Chapter 2:** Total Cost of Ownership vs. Unit Cost...............11

**Chapter 3:** Finding the Right Potential Providers..............19

**Chapter 4:** How to Approach an RFP.............................35

**Chapter 5:** Contents of an Effective RFP ......................51

**Chapter 6:** Financial Business Case............................83

**Chapter 7:** Selecting the Right Partner.......................107

**Chapter 8:** The Contract......................................119

**Chapter 9:** Implementation....................................135

**Chapter 10:** The Sourcing Executive & Sales Executive.........155

**Chapter 11:** Each of Us Has a Job to Do ......................169

Glossary of Terms...............................................175

About the Author................................................179

# INTRODUCTION

For the majority of my career I have been in sales. While I have had stints leading implementation teams, helping to create business units, developing go-to-market strategies, and heading up selling organizations – the root of my professional existence is sales.

It is no secret that in a number of circles there is a stigma associated with any title connected to sales. The reality is a sales position can be defined in many ways. Stereotyping all sales professionals is like assuming that every pro football player is just a football player. Yet we know there are different skill sets, positions and levels of importance of the various players. Individuals and teams will demonstrate fluctuating degrees of quality and skills – both on and off the field. At one end of the spectrum is the sales representative who sells products, or commodities, often looking for a quick hit – with limited required subject matter expertise. On the opposite end is the highly skilled sales executive that works to understand the customer's business requirements and match those up with solutions their company can offer. In the latter, needs are often complex and solutions may be developed as the selling / buying process evolves. While both of these sales resources have value, for the sake of this discussion we will focus on the highly skilled sales executive who presents solutions that are most strategic and somewhat complex to buying organizations.

By my own definition, I am a sales executive. For most of my career I led a team of highly skilled sales professionals focused primarily on helping companies more effectively manage their business communications. The team brought strategic solutions to organizations throughout the United States that solved problems – and created a win-

win for both companies. This business development team concentrated on the most significant and complex opportunities in the organization. As a result, I was involved in leading some of the largest deals structured in the company's history. The long-tenured benefits were recognized by both the company and our customers. In fact, a lot of the developed, cutting-edge solutions became staples of the company's portfolio of offerings. One of the business development executives on our team often referred to the creative solutions and problem solving as exercises that pushed us to become a better company.

The best sales executive title I have seen is Chief Evangelist. I wish I had found that first! Now, after so many years of selling, I have no title on my business card. And, for the past 10 years that my card has been void of one, I have never had anyone ask for it. There is a good reason for this. A title doesn't always effectively convey the only two things customers really want to know:

1. **What is the level of subject matter expertise?** How much does the sales professional know about the customer and their needs; do they have knowledge on how their company's products and services can solve the need?
2. **Does the sales professional have the level of authority to negotiate this deal?** Or, can they corral the resources that can?

For more than 30 years I have been bringing strategic solutions to customers – and learning how the sourcing process works. The opportunities my teams and I have worked on throughout the years have provided me invaluable insight into the world of strategic sourcing. During most of my career I worked for the Standard Register Company. Standard Register is a marketing services and business communications company that serves the financial, healthcare, and general business markets. While originally founded over 100 years ago as a printing company, the organization morphed into providing marketing and business communications solutions that are both printed and electronic with integrated technology being a key component. Standard Register, which has been renamed Taylor Communications, is now part of privately owned Taylor Corporation, one of the largest print and business communications companies in the United States.

Throughout my career, I have attended many sales classes and learned from my mentors on how to strategically sell to some of the best companies out there. Many are Fortune 500 companies. Others are up and coming. Some are small, and destined to remain so, but are powerful businesses. Yet, all have a commonality: problems and needs to be solved. My bosses would like for me to tell you that I strategically navigate around procurement organizations, since many are viewed as sales blockers, and some may not fully understand the business requirements. While this is sometimes true, most of the deals I have worked on involve to some extent the procurement or sourcing team. Regardless of whether a company has a formal sourcing department, every organization has a need to buy materials, products and services. And, not all organizations will utilize a sourcing department to fulfill every buying requirement.

As a sales executive, I have spent so much time working with sourcing that years ago I began studying how organizations make buying decisions. There are some great books that teach how to source. Seminars extend these written materials to provide classroom training on how to become an even better professional sourcing executive. And, consulting firms have built lucrative businesses that solve procurement needs and provide sourcing solutions.

But, what I have not seen much of is a perspective on sourcing from the other side of the table – from someone who has sold the solutions. From a sales executive's point of view, what makes a great deal – for both organizations? What is the process to find the best-fit solution – not just during the vetting period, but long-term such that it benefits your company for years to come? Then, when you find a company you want to partner with, how do you negotiate the best deal – and ensure the implementation yields the results that solve the need associated with the sourcing effort in the first place?

In the following pages I will attempt to answer these questions and provide you with examples of how to accomplish the goals of identifying and implementing an optimal solution for your company – regardless of the need. You will see a methodical process and approach, supported by real-life examples. In the end, you will have the tools to be a better sourcing executive while gaining insight into what goes through the mind of a sales executive.

# 1

# BUYER VS. STRATEGIC SOURCING EXECUTIVE

In the world of sales, we distinctly define the roles of procurement or sourcing as either a buyer or a strategic sourcing executive. The title is not as important as the approach to finding a solution for a need.

A buyer is defined as an individual who sources a product, usually a commodity, looking for the best unit price. The product is often well established, possibly even near the end of its life cycle. For example, let's use notebooks or wooden pencils. Although these products may never be sourced on their own, they will work for demonstration purposes. The likely sales persona servicing this need is the "sales representative" identified in the Introduction.

By contrast, a strategic sourcing executive is someone who looks to solve a problem that falls into one of three areas:

1. A need has arisen that has not previously been sourced, and may not be fully defined.
2. A re-engineering requirement of an existing solution has emerged because the current solution is no longer effective.
3. A solution works, but is not in its ideal state. This may include cost reductions or workflow improvements, beyond solving a need.

The likely sales persona servicing the strategic sourcing executive would be the "sales executive" identified in the Introduction.

The maturity and complexity of a product or solution determines whether the buyer or strategic sourcing executive is involved. And, over time the buying / sourcing resource may change. Generally, the onset of a new solution is more complex than one that has been in place for some time. In this case, a strategic sourcing executive will play a primary role in finding the optimal solution. Once a solution has been in the market for some time, it may become mature and even commoditized. A mature solution often evolves to the point where multiple providers are servicing a saturated market. Most products and solutions follow this growth and life expectancy path. During the process, solutions may hover in between these two ends of the spectrum causing the resource required to become blurred. In these cases, the resource assignment may depend heavily on the requirements of the need, and the services surrounding the fulfillment of the solution.

Where a product or solution falls on the sourcing curve is subject to interpretation. What one company views as a strategic solution, another will consider a commodity. And, it doesn't end with the company seeking the solution. Often the companies selling solutions will view their own products and services differently as they compete. Thus, aligning with potential providers on how you both view the required services is critical in determining who will be your provider of choice.

The sourcing curve below demonstrates a product or solution's life with an overlay of who may become involved in selecting the right solution.

A key differentiator of a strategic sourcing executive is that they will include the business owner in the buying process. Sometimes these are the same resource but often, the strategic sourcing executive is part of a specific procurement or sourcing department. When the lines of business, or business owner and the sourcing executive align, it often results in a successful search for the right solution. The business owner will fully understand the requirements of the need, while the strategic sourcing executive will have the time and acumen to find potential solutions available in the marketplace.

**Figure 1.1 – Sourcing Curve: Strategic Sourcing Executive vs. Buyer**

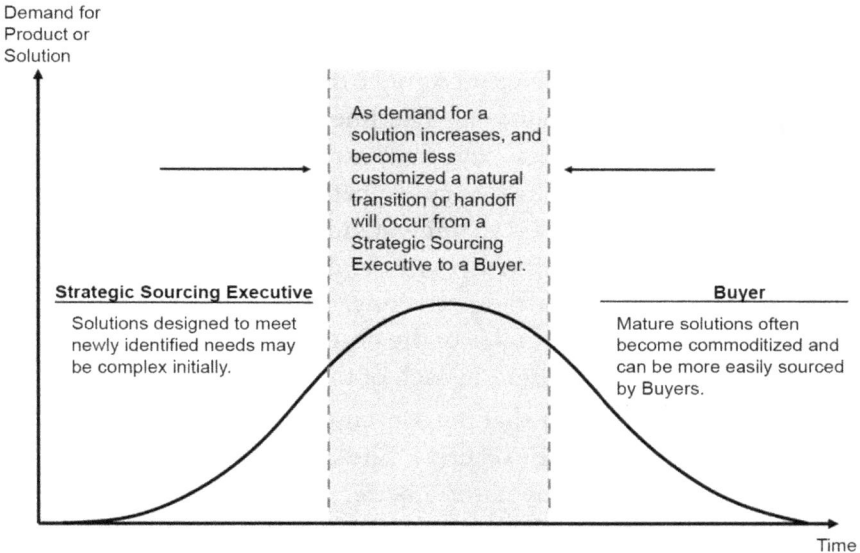

Demand for
Product or
Solution

As demand for a solution increases, and become less customized a natural transition or handoff will occur from a Strategic Sourcing Executive to a Buyer.

**Strategic Sourcing Executive**

Solutions designed to meet newly identified needs may be complex initially.

**Buyer**

Mature solutions often become commoditized and can be more easily sourced by Buyers.

Time

There can be disconnects when the sourcing professional and business are not aligned. Sometimes this is created because the "owner" of the initiative is not well defined. When there is a separate sourcing department, cooperation from both teams is essential to ensuring a successful solution. There must also be demonstrated or proven value to the business. Otherwise, procurement or sourcing is seen as a barrier, making a solution difficult to reach. I cannot tell you how many times I have seen sourcing initiatives fail because of disagreements between the business and the sourcing department.

A case in point involved a complex sale my team and I were working on for an international wealth management firm. They wanted their agents and brokers to be able to go on-line, via a custom portal and personalize business communications and sales collateral to use with prospective clients. The available materials needed to include some static pieces about the investment market and firm, as well as customized materials specific to an individual client. The portal would house templates and building components that would allow an agent or broker to print materials locally or in a centralized facility, and provide the materials electronically as needed – for email or electronic presentations.

The customer and my team agreed the need was for a strategic and highly customized solution. The line of business, who managed the existing, manual process and their strategic sourcing department were involved in the initiative to find a better solution. We frequently met with the line of business to understand the current state and begin building a solution. The intensity of the discovery and solution build often included white-boarding sessions, demonstrations of varying technology and prototype builds of the potential solution. A member of the sourcing team was present in each of these sessions as well.

It quickly became clear that the sourcing team member was a buyer, and not a strategic sourcing executive. She knew little about the business – its current state or the need for a better solution. In most meetings she would add comments that were off topic or clearly indicated she was not capable of strategically driving the solution.

Although she was unqualified, she advised that once the solution was determined, she would be negotiating terms to ensure we provided the best price available. It was clear that she did not understand the solution being developed and thus, would be incapable of negotiating a fair market price.

The misalignment between sourcing and the business presented challenges that could have been avoided. As a result of the wrong sourcing resource being assigned, the business carried the entire burden of fulfilling the needs of the initiative. During the engagement, my team agreed that the process might have been better managed if the right resources were assigned and better aligned within the customer's organization.

The skill set of the strategic sourcing executive is beyond that of the buyer. But, this does not mean the buyer isn't an essential resource.

One of my customers, a chief procurement officer at a large southeast regional bank, once discussed these two polar opposite roles within her organization. She was new to the bank and, although she had come from a similar position in the northeast, adjusting to the culture of a southern bank was a big challenge. The chief procurement officer was laser-focused on reinventing the bank's approach to sourcing – the reason she was hired in the first place.

Prior to her joining the bank, I had been matched up with one of the buyers in her organization that thought of himself as a strategic sourcing executive. But, he was a buyer. No matter the need, he approached everything as a buyer would:

- I'll add you to the bid list.
- What's your cost?
- Leave your card on the desk.

As someone who sells strategic solutions, being matched up with a buyer is a death sentence – both for me and the customer. Not only do I lose when matched up to a buyer, but the company who needs my solutions will never know what they've missed out on. To make matters worse, my company had some history with this buyer that left a poor impression of us. When I say "some history" it was a 10-year-old issue with an account manager, who was no longer with our company.

When I mentioned this to the chief sourcing officer, she acknowledged my concerns, admitted that he was not a strategic sourcing executive, and that we were inappropriately matched. She did however, point out that buyers do serve a critical purpose in the world of sourcing. The needs of the bank were such that some buys were strategic, while others were not. Having tactical, commodity buyers ensured that mature products and services were sourced only from the best companies at the best available prices. When the need was more complex and strategic to the bank, the commodity buyer would never be able to find and source the solution. This is where a strategic sourcing executive is critical. I could not agree more.

The challenge many companies face is knowing when to deploy a buying approach vs. strategic sourcing. Compounding this problem are buyers trying to function as strategic sourcing executives. On the other side of the table, sales representatives and executives must know the difference between their own offerings – commodity vs. strategic. Like the procurement or sourcing organization, the company selling its goods and services has to know when to assign a sales representative versus a sales executive.  When strategic sourcing is required, and there is an alignment of the teams – the experience can be rewarding in fulfilling the need with an optimal solution.

———————————————

# Key Points

- A buyer is an individual who sources a specific product, usually a commodity, looking for the best price.  The product is often well established, possibly near the end of its life cycle.
- A strategic sourcing executive looks to solve a problem where a need has arisen that has not previously been sourced or fully defined, a re-engineering requirement of an existing solution has emerged, and/or the company is looking to optimize a solution that works, but is not in its ideal state.
- As demand for a solution increases, becomes more mature and less customized a natural transition from a strategic sourcing executive to a buyer will occur.
- The challenge many companies face is in knowing when to deploy a buying approach vs. strategic sourcing.

# 2
# TOTAL COST OF OWNERSHIP VS. UNIT COST

When addressing a company's needs, the frequent goal of many sourcing exercises is to reduce operating expenses while improving revenue. This often goes hand-in-hand with identifying a solution for a specific need. Many companies take a tactical approach and attempt to reduce spending by negotiating the unit cost. Although an important aspect, it is not always the most optimal method of addressing a need. And, in the larger picture, it may be only one piece of the total cost of ownership.

Understanding the true costs of your need, including non-product related costs, is essential to building a comprehensive strategy to yield the most significant savings or return on investment. On average, I believe unit price is less than 20% of the total cost of ownership. Many organizations focus on the 20%, tip of the iceberg – ignoring process costs such as design, workflow, technology, and logistics, which can make up nearly 80% of the cost. The unit cost is easy to see, put in a spreadsheet and evaluate in comparison to the current state and other potential providers. Whereas, costs outside of the unit are more challenging to define and tend to "sit below the waterline."

**Figure 2.1 – Total Cost of Ownership Iceberg**

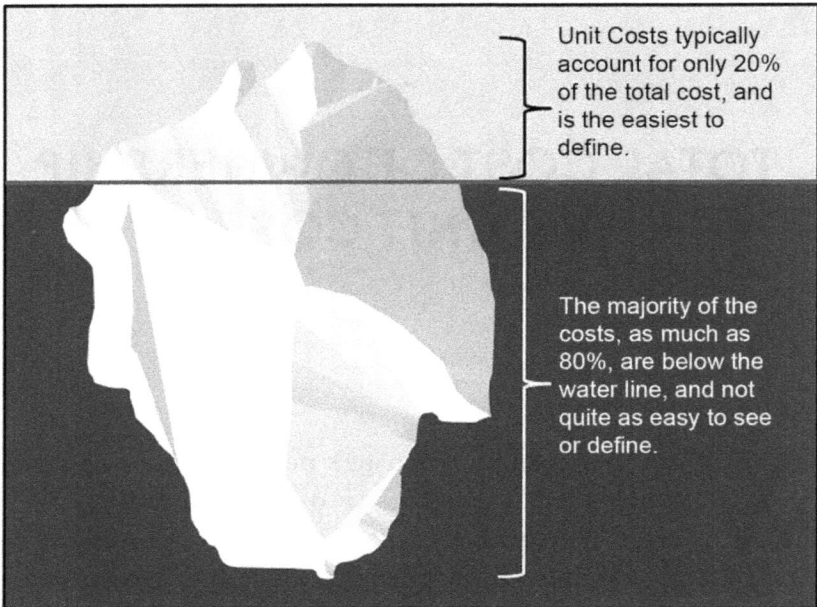

Unit Costs typically account for only 20% of the total cost, and is the easiest to define.

The majority of the costs, as much as 80%, are below the water line, and not quite as easy to see or define.

# Strategic Approach – Total Cost of Ownership

As challenging as it may seem, needs requiring strategic solutions demand more than a just a unit cost discount. They require a total cost of ownership approach, well beyond the cost of a particular unit or product.

A strategic approach forces an evaluation of the optimal solution, beyond costs that are easily visible. This includes how the solution will be used, the workflow impact, and reducing product consumption.

Suppose a strategic solution shrinks the labor effort required to perform the tasks and fulfill the need. Those resources can be redeployed, thus reducing the overall cost – while improving other areas of the organization. The optimal solution may also dramatically improve the workflow, allowing the company to deliver faster, and more reliably.

Imagine the financial impact if the optimal solution reduces the time it takes to get to market, or the number of sales days outstanding on its accounts receivables. Or, what if the solution encourages reduced consumption of the product? For instance, instead of a price reduction on printed materials, you make a switch to electronic media.

What if a solution is more expensive, but positively impacts revenue? I have seen scenarios where a solution may increase costs but, drives increased revenues. Perhaps this is why marketing organizations are less concerned with spending money than with procurement departments. Unless the solution is highly commoditized, a unit price discount rarely delivers total savings or a positive return on investment.

**Current Unit Price – Negotiated Market Discount ≠ Total Savings**

In a strategic buy the total cost of ownership approach is most effective because it aligns the goals of the customer with its business partner. It also encourages an organization to buy only what is needed – at the most competitive rates.

For example, let's assume an organization spends $10 million annually on business communications. A due diligence exercise may uncover a potential 20% decrease in spending. Although unit cost may be a contributing factor, the larger contributors are process improvements, logistics efficiencies (i.e. packaging and shipping), and effective consumption management. The optimal solution needs to include a measurable way of tracking performance to ensure the organization achieves the financial target. Detailed reporting on cost of ownership and the migration process are key, as they provide an opportunity to tweak the implemented solution if necessary.

# Tactical Approach – Unit Cost Model

A unit cost model focuses exclusively on a snapshot in time of the need – anticipating that it will not significantly change in the future. In this process, the most aggressive unit price is negotiated. This can be an effective model when the solution is a mature commodity. However, it rarely yields overall financial benefit if the need requires a more strategic solution.

Today, more than ever before, organizations find their business requirements changing rapidly. The specifications of strategic solutions change at an even faster pace. Because of these two factors, the unit cost model may appear attractive even in a strategic buy at first, but then becomes obsolete almost immediately afterwards.

Using the previous example of a $10 million spend, a unit cost model may look at all of the products that comprise a spend – or as many as can be identified, spec'd out and priced in the market. The exercise may demonstrate aggressive price reductions on the individual products that total a very inviting savings. However, the organization has to assume the solution really is commoditized and that no significant spec or demand changes will occur over the course of the program. Otherwise, there is no guarantee that long-term savings will be found over the current spend.

In a strategic buy, a unit cost model creates competing objectives between the client and business partner. The client may want to decrease overall spending, yet the business partner is incentivized to sell as much product as possible at a discounted price. What the partner cannot earn in gross margin is exchanged for sheer volume.

A buyer will almost always focus on unit price, whereas a strategic sourcing executive looks for the best overall solution, inclusive of a positive return on investment. Most senior executives will also focus on the overall value to the organization, as opposed to the tactical cost components. This same effect can be realized when outside consulting firms assist in the sourcing process. However, even sophisticated consulting firms may view certain solutions as commodities, and deploy a buyer's approach – while others define the need as more strategic, and will utilize a strategic sourcing methodology. Problems may arise if the assessment of the need is inaccurate, which may mean a unit cost model approach is used when the need warrants a strategic sourcing effort.

While there may be multiple reasons for the misalignment, it is most often caused when a unit price model is inappropriately used because it's an easy way to compare two or more competing offers, side by side. However, just because it's easy does not mean the comparative offers will solve your need.

When a well-known consulting firm issued a Request for Proposal (RFP) on behalf of a commercial bank, I responded. We had a good relationship with the bank and believed we could bring strategic value to the defined need. During our presentation, the consulting firm was largely focused on the unit cost of various products – as opposed to the total cost of ownership, and overall financial improvement we offered. Specifically, our model encouraged the purchase of fewer products, at higher unit costs, while still guaranteeing the client more substantial savings. I contended that dramatically lowering unit costs to a point where my margins were unattractive was not only bad for my company, but it encouraged unnecessary buys of products just because the unit price was cheap. In addition, the consulting firm wanted us to offer the bank incentives for spending more dollars with my company and even asked for additional discounts as part of a longer term contract. This was out-of-sync with their client's needs. I was being incentivized to sell a higher volume of products and the client was being encouraged to buy products they simply did not need.

I engaged the consultants in a discussion about why they thought great unit costs and incentives would bring value to the strategic solution their client was looking for. I then drew the following chart on the whiteboard.

## Figure 2.2 – Unit Cost vs. Total Cost of Ownership

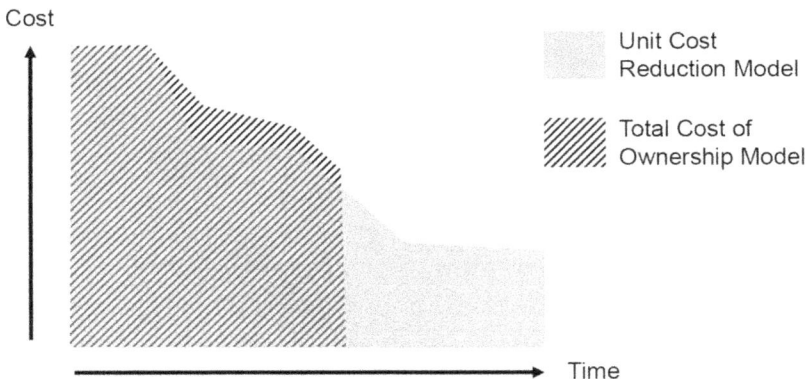

The effect of the unit cost over time is represented by the solid light gray area. Whereas, the total cost of ownership model is represented by the striped darker gray lines. The area contained in each respective model represents dollars consumed. As you can see, despite a common objective, there is a distinct difference in how each model performs over time.

The unit cost model relied on a triple discount – a decrease in the current cost, an additional discount for increased spend, and a length of contract reward. And, there was no incentive for either party to consider less consumption or alternative channels of communications that were less costly.

By contrast, the total cost of ownership model contained a capped spend approach with targeted solutions that encouraged less consumption and a shift away from more expensive products. This model offered the bank better cost savings with a decrease in overall spending – even in scenarios where the unit cost may go up. The assumption being, the least expensive product was the one the bank never had to buy.

Because the need required a strategic solution, the total cost of ownership was the best model and, our solution was selected by the bank. The consultant even agreed that his emphasis on the unit cost approach was misguided in this situation.

You may be wondering what the incentive is to sell less products and services to a customer. It's really very simple. In a unit cost model, the supplier has very little mark-up in product cost, and replaces thin gross margins with overall volume. By contrast, a total cost of ownership focuses less on the unit cost and more on the total cost of the spend. So, while there may not be as much revenue, the products and services sold have a nice gross margin associated with them. Companies survive by turning profits … not by generating revenue. If I don't offer this strategic approach, I am just another sales representative pushing products without the long-term, best interests of my customers in mind. The total cost of ownership provides the best of both worlds – the customer gains an affordable solution, often with a reduction in spending and I make a nice margin. Win-win.

While unit cost models have their place it is critical that needs requiring strategic solutions are approached with a total cost of ownership mindset. Understanding the difference between the two models and when to use them can be challenging. When defining a need and its potential solutions, a thorough examination should be conducted as to which model is the best fit. While there is no textbook way to determine this, selecting the right model will ensure the stability of the solution and a sustainable return on investment.

———————————

# Key Points

- Understanding the true costs of a need, the current state and recommended solution, including non-product related costs, is essential to building a comprehensive strategy that will yield the most significant cost savings or return on investment.

- Most companies focus on unit price even though process costs often make up nearly 80% of the total cost, offering a better opportunity for overall savings.

- Needs requiring strategic solutions demand more than a unit cost discount approach. These solutions require a total cost of ownership approach, which is well beyond the final cost of a particular unit or product.

- Unless the solution to a need is highly commoditized, a favorably discounted unit price from the current state spend rarely delivers total savings or a positive return on investment.

# 3
# FINDING THE RIGHT POTENTIAL PROVIDERS

When a company has needs that require outsourced solutions, the biggest challenge can be finding the right partners. The reasons can be varied but some might include:

- The need is not well-defined, and thus cannot be easily explained to potential providers.
- There is an inability to identify subject matter expertise in providing the right solution.
- Finding potential providers in the marketplace may be challenging.
- It is difficult to find a partner that can be trusted, creating risk.

New issues and changing demands will have companies constantly looking for providers to address needs that have not been required before.

There are four key approaches to finding the right potential partner: research on your own, engage with a trusted partner, discuss with other potential providers, and when required – issue a Request for Information (RFI). It is important to note that these approaches are not intended to be alternatives – but, rather an inclusion of the three or four.

## Figure 3.1 – Process to Find the Optimal Partner Pool

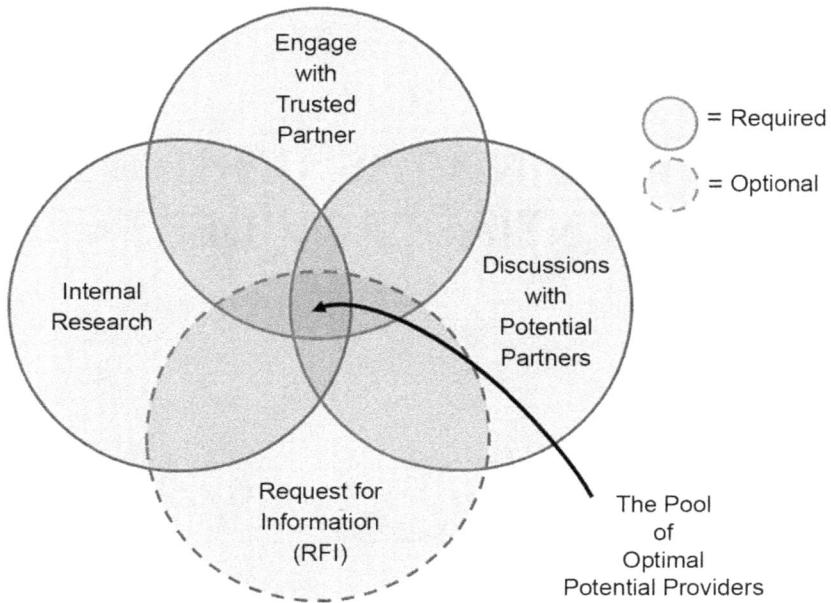

Depending on the scope of the need, you may decide to skip the formal RFI and/or subsequent RFP. To determine a go-forward strategy, you may want to combine internal research and your discussions with potential partners. In either case internal research and conversations involving potential partners should be included.

# Internal Research

Do your homework. Study the market, learn what is available, and reach out to your peers. If you do not take the time to research potential providers and their capabilities – inclusive of how your peers may have solved similar problems, then be prepared to be taken for a wild ride. When you opt to learn everything directly from providers, you must know that they may not have your best interests at heart. For example, a provider may be working to solve a problem that is more closely aligned with its solutions or products as opposed to your specific needs. You have to be able to recognize this before getting in too deep.

Researching the market can be daunting. But, with the tools available today – you have never had more information right at your fingertips. Use the internet to learn as much as you can about providers in the industry, their strengths and weaknesses, and their methodology for implementing solutions. Most reputable providers will have this information available on their websites.

Almost every company today has peer groups – or organizations with similar products and services. These companies can be brought together by industry associations or networking opportunities. Reach out to these resources and float your situation by them. Chances are fairly good that they have had, or currently have, a similar problem, and may have already solved it! Even competitors may be willing to discuss how they have solved problems. And these can be some of your best resources.

# Engage with a Trusted Partner

Consider engaging a current, trusted partner. Since you already have a successful business relationship, use them if you can. Even if the situation is slightly different, you will likely still find this to be a good resource.

Engaging with a trusted partner can benefit you in a couple of ways. First, it provides a level of confidence that you won't have with new providers, as they have already proven themselves capable of assisting you in solving other needs. Second, even if they are not able to develop a solution for this particular need, they may be able to recommend other potential providers. In a best case scenario, the trusted partner will be able to address your need, saving you the time it takes to find a new source. This may seem like an easy way out. But, if the objective is to solve a need, it makes sense to chase the solution that is easiest and quickest to implement – while yielding the results both you and the trusted partner expect.

# Discussions with Potential Partners

One of the largest missed opportunities in finding potential partners is having open and honest dialog with the provider community. Why this is the case, has always been a mystery to me. I suppose, sometimes there are legitimate concerns for avoiding direct contact with potential providers, such as protection of intellectual property or confidential information. In these cases, work to provide a mechanism where open dialog can occur. The benefit of having these conversations will often far outweigh any risk or negative outcome.

Having open and honest dialog means sharing as much about your situation as you can with potential partners. Invite them to have discussions with you and the decision making team, allowing time for a question and answer session. Depending on the complexity of the need, consider including a high-level white-boarding session as well.

Part of this conversation means being candid about your need. You can always ask a potential partner if they can provide a specific product or solution that you may have discovered on your own. However, consider allowing them to make recommendations. Even if you think you know the solution, you may discover a better one by having these kinds of discussions. Give potential partners a chance to help solve the problem. Unless you are up for a misfired solution, there is no value in keeping your business need a secret.

One of the best laid-out and managed opportunities I worked on was for a services organization that supported credit unions. One of the solutions they provided was documents and selling aids for various member credit unions. These included sell sheets, marketing materials, loan applications, and signature cards. The process was highly manual and with each new credit union, there was a time consuming onboarding process. The service provider was looking to automate the process – which included making broad-sweeping document updates across multiple credit unions. The business requirements and rules were so complicated that we realized developing an optimal solution was beyond our capabilities, and removed ourselves from further consideration.

The best part of the experience was the process they used, particularly in the early phase, to find potential partners. In the beginning stage, they invited the potential providers to two workshops to ensure we understood their current state and need. The first was an all-day session where the service provider shared their onboarding and workflow processes for a newly landed credit union, as well as how they manage changes for existing customers. All of the potential providers attended this first session together, and while initially a bit awkward, most warmed to the situation by midday. The second session, held a couple of weeks later, was a one-on-one with each potential provider, allowing us the opportunity to ask questions and to have more candid conversations since our competitors were not in the room. By using these two sessions, the service provider gained a working view of the potential partners. They could actually see the level of subject matter expertise unfold in the sessions. At the same time, the potential providers could evaluate their ability to provide an optimal solution. This was in fact, when we decided our company was not a good fit, and withdrew from the process – saving a significant amount of money on what could have been a long process to determine we were not the right partner.

Another key benefit of having open and honest conversations is the ability to connect with Subject Matter Experts (SMEs) within each of the potential providers. While sales executives know a certain amount of information, most will bring along one or more SMEs to discuss the details of a particular solution, which can help build confidence in them. In addition, these conversations allow you to connect with the individuals who have the detailed knowledge and experience of similar solutions that have been deployed with other clients.

We have an internal process where we meet prior to bringing a SME in front of a customer. This allows us the opportunity to bring the SME up to speed – and to evaluate how they will perform in front of the customer. You can expect that every potential provider is going through a similar process to ensure they are bringing the absolute best SMEs to the table. It is worth your time to ask the potential providers their process to select SMEs, and their backgrounds, prior to meeting them for the first time.

This approach will take some time – but it is time well invested in learning the players in the marketplace and knowing if you have the right potential providers to help build the solution you actually need.

# Request for Information

After finding a pool of potential providers, a logical next step may be to issue a formal RFI. This is your opportunity to begin vetting the potential providers beyond just knowing if they play in the space and through your discovery conversations. In order to make the most of an RFI, ensure the requested information is meaningful and provides answers that will help you decide which providers you want to include for further consideration.

In simple terms, ask only the questions to which you most want the answers. Larry King was often asked why he was such a successful interviewer. His response was that he asked questions which he and others wanted answered. An RFI should do the same thing. Don't get caught up in asking questions that will not benefit you in making a decision – just because they sound amazing! At this stage, you are looking for potential providers to help recommend alternative solutions. So, only ask the questions that will help you make a decision!

I am always surprised when customers ask me for a list of potential questions to include in an RFI or RFP. In some situations, I have even been asked to provide sample RFIs and RFPs to be used in sourcing exercises. The best RFIs and RFPs I have received are those where my solution was selected as the winning bid. However, that doesn't always mean they were the most well written documents or that they contained really great and probing questions.

If you don't know the questions to ask – and a potential provider gives them to you, you are not going to know what to do with the answers when you get them. Do your homework, avoid putting yourself in this situation and never ask a potential provider for a list of questions.

I should point out that certain highly technical needs may include detailed specifications you do have to obtain from the potential providers. As an example, sourcing for the building of an aircraft may involve highly technical information that only the provider community can effectively provide.

As you build an RFI, remember that the objective at this stage is to help you identify potential providers that you can invite in for deeper conversations. Since every business requirement and subsequent sourcing scenario is unique, there is no way to provide a sample of a best-in-class RFI. I have however, created a list of categories that will help you build an RFI that works in most situations.

- **Describe the Current State.** Outline your current situation to the potential providers. This should be a description of the specific need you are trying to solve. You should share a fairly in-depth description of the current state, including workflow diagrams that show the process as it exists today. Keep in mind, the more you share the better the responses.

- **Process for Making a Decision.** Give the potential providers some guidance as to what your process will be. Since this is likely a discovery exercise you may not know all of the details. But, you should have an idea that an RFP may be issued, solution build will occur, presentations / meetings will be held, etc. The more you can tell the prospective providers, the more serious they will take your request.

- **Demographic Information.** You may have already done this but, be sure you capture information on the provider's background, their leadership profile, and organizational structure. It is also important to know their financial stability as you will not want to engage with a partner whose business is overshadowed by financial concerns.

- **Service Offerings.** Ask for a description of products and services that address the current state situation.

- **Process for Building a Solution.** What steps need to take place to reach an optimal solution? Is there a workflow diagram on how the potential provider approaches solution development?

- **Subject Matter Expertise.** Who are the individuals that would help solve the need? What are their backgrounds? How are resources hired and trained?

- **Implementation.** How will the business be managed during the implementation and afterwards? Are different teams used to implement vs. manage the on-going account relationship? You will want to ensure there is subject matter expertise during and after the implementation.

- **Approach for Building a Pricing Model.** Since an RFI is generally not a detailed pricing exercise (this is saved for later – such as during an RFP), ask the potential providers to give some guidance on how pricing is approached. This may include such things as time and materials, cost-plus model, programming fees, management fees, etc.

- **Case Studies.** Ask for examples of similar work completed for other customers. Ensure these are actual client implementations that can be referenced if asked.

- **Customer References.** These should focus on similar solutions for other clients. You may be inclined to only look for experience in a similar industry but, don't get too hung up on this. The best strategy may come from a provider that has never worked in your market.

- **Distinction in Marketplace.** What makes this provider better than the others?

Remember, only ask the questions that will help you make your decision. Part of this may involve putting yourself in the position of the sales executive and asking yourself how you might answer the posed questions or requests. Two examples of poor questions come to mind:

1. Who do you consider to be your competitors?
2. Please provide references of customers you have lost.

If you do not know who my competitors are, I am probably not going to list any that I would want to face when trying to win your business. I have to assume that if I give you the name of a competitor you did not include in the RFI – there is a possibility that at some point they will appear in the game. Do your homework and determine who the players are in the space. If for some reason you cannot uncover the competitive landscape in your research, use the open and honest conversations to help flesh this out.

For as long as I can remember I have been providing bankrupt companies who have ceased operations or businesses that have been sold as my list of lost customer references. This answers the question. But, it really provides no material value since it will be difficult to contact a company in either of these scenarios. And, the fact is few potential providers will supply a list of lost customers that you may actually be able to contact. Let's face it, every business loses customers at some point. It is generally not a pretty thing, and in many cases the loss was caused by poor customer service, oversold commitments, or complacency; and, not always a flawed solution. Occasionally the customer has outgrown the provider or its business requirements have changed. In any of these situations, a potential provider isn't going to risk a valued opportunity or their reputation by allowing you to speak with someone who will tell you anything other than how great they are. Bottom line, you will not gain any insight from attempting to contact a lost customer.

# Culture

Cultural compatibility is the single most important element in selecting a partner. In fact, it extends beyond the compatibility of the organizations and into the recommended solution, but, is not a measurable criterion. Even though it is the most critical element – there is no way to objectively measure how well you and the potential partner can work together.

The worst outcome of finding the right partner is uncovering that the best possible solution cannot be implemented because of the culture of your own organization, or the lack of compatibility with the selected partner.

Most of the lost opportunities I've been involved in are due to the company not selecting a partner and solution; rather choosing to operate with the status quo. Part of your homework is to determine if your company has the cultural appetite to change from its current state. In fact, this should be done before you begin searching for a solution or engaging potential partners.

The decision to stay with the status quo may be due to a solution being more invasive than anticipated. Sometimes you don't know this until you get started but, try to keep top of mind the impact a selected solution may have on your organization. In doing so, you specifically want to know if your company can handle the cultural impact of changing to a recommended solution.

As much as I don't want to admit it, I have lost opportunities to cultural incompatibility. For years I thought my charm and intellect allowed me everything necessary to work with any company. Unfortunately, not every solution provider can work with potential customers. It may not be as personal as I once thought though – it may be that culturally the two companies are not aligned or that the recommended solution involves more change than the customer can handle. It is as much the sales executive's role as yours to make this determination early in the process. Neither party wants to waste time building and presenting a solution when the companies are just not in sync with each other. Cut the ties early in the game if you get the sense it isn't going to work. And, know that it is ok to share this as the reason for separation.

Some of the greatest fails are those seemingly optimal solutions that just cannot be implemented. And, often culture is the culprit. For years I have listened to senior executives talk about great strategies that failed because they were not effectively implemented. When this occurs, it is frequently the result of strategies that are stymied by culture. And, frankly, if a strategy cannot be implemented – then the strategy itself is flawed.

As Dick Clark, former Merck CEO once said, "Culture eats strategy for lunch." However, there are some things you can do to uncover the cultural effect:

- Ask yourself, how much change can your company handle?
- Share your cultural limitations with potential providers.
- Engage in interactive discussions.
- Ask for solution ideas to test their fit.
- Push the cultural boundaries of your company.

As our company was working on a Business Process Outsourcing (BPO) solution for a national retail bank, we bumped into cultural boundaries a few times. To complicate things, at the same time, the bank was transforming into a single brand, after a merger combined three individual banks.

Part of the solution involved a recommended technology platform that could not interface with the bank's existing infrastructure. The problem was that it could not talk to our platform (or, anyone else's for that matter) in an automated process. Without the interface, it would require a manual intervention that would mean additional human resources on the part of any potential provider, to handle the volume. This would result in increased costs to the bank.

When we presented this concern to the sourcing executive leading the team, he immediately shut us down. He made the comment, "This decision has been made and we will use only the bank's technology." This declaration was made having never explored how our technology could be advantageous to his business. It was clear that the proverbial cultural barrier had been erected.

Privately, one of the key members of our sales team approached the sourcing executive and asked if he could demonstrate our technology platform so he could see the mutual benefits in detail. He agreed and, after that demo, a lengthy conversation, and some follow-up meetings the bank finally agreed to move away from their outdated technology platform.

While there were a number of factors that likely played into the sourcing executive's initial hard and fast stance regarding the bank's existing technology, I believe both of us could agree culture was the leading issue. Clearly the decision to move away from the bank's technology was a bold shift for their conservative organization – but in the end it proved to be the right solution. The cultural barrier was removed.

As you work to find a group of potential partners, resist the temptation to include only those you or others in your company know. It can be very limiting and may not offer the most robust solution. Stretch yourself to include suppliers you have never worked with. Even if you end up going with a familiar provider, the information you gain will be invaluable – and may even help you with future sourcing initiatives.

# What is the Sales Executive Thinking?

While you are trying to narrow the playing field of potential partners, sales leaders are working equally as hard to ensure their efforts are yielding sold solutions. I constantly evaluate whether we should pursue an opportunity based on the odds of having the winning solution. Early in the process I ask myself these three questions:

1. Have I met the decision maker (the business owner, not the sourcing executive)?
2. Is there an opportunity early on to meet with the business team and discuss the current state?
3. Do I have a relationship with the decision maker?

If I cannot answer "yes" to all three questions, I will withdraw. If you were me, would you chase deals where the decision maker or current operations team were not engaged? I know from experience that without having satisfied these three questions, my chances of winning a deal are about as likely as buying a winning million-dollar lottery ticket. From the first point of contact to the end of a sale, I will spend up to $200,000. These costs become part of the sell price that all of my customers will ultimately bear. Since there is a limit to how much I can pass on to customers, my probability of winning has to be better than the lottery odds.

One of the largest deals sold in my company's history (and my own personal career) was to an educational financial services company who solicited and serviced student loans. The initial contact came when the customer called our call center for information about our services. When I later spoke with the contact, he was extremely open about their current process and how growth in recent years had affected their ability to continue internally managing the business. I asked him to spend some time telling me what they were currently doing and allow me to meet the project sponsor/business owner. My request was very well received and I began building a relationship with one of the key decision makers. This was my assurance that we would likely agree to move forward.

What if this conversation had not provided a "yes" to the three questions, and we had withdrawn? Imagine the potential loss to that company. Now put yourself in a position where you decide not to share information relative to the three questions. What if a potential provider has the absolute best solution – but you never find out because your process got in the way? Adhering to a process at the expense of vetting the right providers will not just waste your time and that of the potential partners, it could cost you the best overall outcome.

Be careful creating a feeding frenzy that invites potential providers to a party that never creates a "win" – particularly if you go back to the well too often without any meaningful reward.

For a number of years, I sold to a consulting firm that sourced solutions on behalf of companies who were revamping their procurement organizations. During this time, I lost every deal presented. Even when I had what I believed to be the best solution, I never won. Finally, I learned my lesson and advised the managing partner I would no longer work on any opportunity from their firm. After 10 years of consistently losing, I knew I simply could not continue to invest in their deals. Aiding in my decision was the fact that these opportunities were considerably more invasive on my team's time and our company's financial resources; more so than most other deals in which we participated. It cost our company a lot of money and lost productivity before I finally made that tough decision. And, for a period of time, many in my own organization could not believe I was walking away from such intriguing opportunities. The consulting firm doubted my ability to stay away for long, too. So, for a few years they continued sending me and others in my company opportunities. After a lot of "no's" thankfully, we no longer hear from them.

A worthwhile exercise might be to look back on past sourcing decisions you have been part of – particularly ones that didn't go so well, and ask yourself how you handled the first two questions above. And, did you allow yourself to build a relationship with the potential providers?

The objective early in the process is to find potential partners who can help you with a specific problem. But, there are limits to how much you should ask of a provider when you cannot give them any level of assurance you will be moving forward together. Most providers have boundaries on how much they will share for free. Be respectful of this, and know there is a different process for moving deep into solution development – which often comes with a price tag.

I learned a valuable lesson from a New England-based consulting firm on how to address this very problem. At the time, my company was exploring the possibility of creating a consulting firm – as a new business unit. Since I had previously worked on a number of occasions with the New England firm, I suggested to my boss that we go visit the principal owner. This would be a good opportunity to pick her brain and gain a better understanding of how she started her own business. It was an effort to learn and hopefully avoid a few pitfalls. Fortunately, the principal agreed to spend an entire day with us – free of charge!

When we first arrived at their headquarters, she entered the conference room with a presence that exuded professionalism and subject matter expertise. I knew we had landed in the right spot to test our business plan.

She spent the first few minutes listening to me present and then we discussed our business plan. I brought documents, a PowerPoint® presentation and workflow diagrams. We even shared target market information and the results of a couple of focus group studies.

After a few minutes, she interrupted with some softball questions. Then she got tougher. At one point, I thought I was on 60 Minutes. But, I appreciated the spirit with which she was providing input. Since we had successfully worked with this firm in the past, we both wanted a positive outcome from the meeting.

However, once she took control of the meeting, she used a very consistent approach in the discussions. By now, she had invited some of her team to participate, and they began offering recommendations on how to improve our model. That was met with follow-up questions from my boss and me. Her team would answer a couple of the follow-ups … but, then the principal would cut off the conversation. She would say, "Additional information on that topic will need to be in the form of a paid engagement." By the end of the day we were reciting the line in unison.

That taught me an important lesson. There is merit in sharing subject matter expertise in order to establish credibility. But, there is a point when continuing to give away free information isn't going to help me close the deal. And, in most cases it is unnecessary. I often find myself repeating the consultant's line to my own customers, when I am being pressed for information that I feel is a bit too far.

---

# Key Points

- There are four key approaches to finding the right potential partner:
    - Engage with an existing trusted partner
    - Research on your own
    - Talk openly and honestly with potential providers
    - Issue a Request for Information (RFI), which is optional
- When you decide to use an RFI, remember that the objective at this stage in the process is to help you identify the potential providers that you can invite in for deeper conversations.

There are several components worth considering to ensure you have an effective RFI:

- Describe the current state
- Share the process for making a decision
- Require demographic information
- Ask for service offerings
- Inquire about the process for building a solution
- Understand subject matter expertise
- Explain the implementation process
- Define the approach for building a pricing model
- Ask for case studies
- Require customer references
- Ask for their distinction in the marketplace

- The cultural compatibility of your organization and that of the potential provider is the single most important element in selecting a partner.
- As you are working to narrow the playing field of potential partners, sales leaders are working equally as hard to ensure their efforts are yielding sold solutions. Three criteria that a sales executive will often use to determine if continuing to pursue an opportunity is worthwhile:
  - Have they met the decision maker?
  - Is there an opportunity early on to meet with the business team and discuss the current state situation?
  - Is there a relationship with the decision maker (or team), or can one be built that will influence the decision?
- Understand that most credible potential partners will have a limit on how much information they are willing to share for free.

# 4
# HOW TO APPROACH AN RFP

Now that you have identified the potential providers, the next step is to narrow the field to the provider or providers you will choose to solve the need. While there are other approaches, this often means issuing a Request for Proposal (RFP) to the potential providers.

For many in the sales world, an RFP is met with dread and reluctance. This may have something to do with the lengthy process in store. Or maybe, it's because the odds of being selected are simply not favorable.

## Do You Need a Request for Proposal?

There is a good chance that at some point, you have questioned yourself as to whether there is even a need for an RFP. Why go down the path of issuing an RFP? Believe me, there are sales executives all across the country who ask themselves the same thing. It seems there are times when the solution and partner are so obvious that an RFP only delays the inevitable, and wastes a lot of time.

Whenever I question the rationale, the response I frequently get is, "That's our company policy", or, "We want to test the market." Neither of which is a great reason to continue with an RFP if you believe you already know the solution and the best potential partner.

Oftentimes, a company knows what they need to do, and it becomes apparent to the potential providers what is likely to happen. And, the sourcing team's focus shifts from trying to vet potential solutions to protecting the choice they want to make. It is ok to identify the optimal solution early in the process and with whom you want to work. But, end the process – and don't go to RFP simply because that is what you're supposed to do.

"Testing the market" is an interesting phrase and can mean a lot of different things. It can range from checking competitive prices to seeing the options that are available, to discovering new players in the market. But, if there is no intent to change your current course or if the likelihood of using a new solution is remote, this can be a frustrating exercise. Everyone is busy with their day-to-day jobs. So, to be pulled off for an exercise in futility can be frustrating both for you and the potential providers. When there is little to no intention of selecting a new solution, it is time consuming and expensive for everyone involved.

Now, suppose your senior executives task you with a reduction of 15% on all current contracts. If you are satisfied with your providers, and your only objective is to drive spend down, go meet with them! Candidly tell them what is going on, and most times, you will receive a positive reaction, without going through the RFP process. Current providers have zero interest in responding to a costly RFP to protect their business. In fact, many would gladly offer you a discount to avoid it.

Imagine the time saved and immediate benefit your company can receive by simply renegotiating the current programs. RFPs can be invasive, costly, time-consuming, and a lengthy process to recognize the potential value, or return on investment.

Sometimes the RFP process eliminates some of the best potential providers. As I mentioned earlier, some providers choose to withdraw from opportunities simply on the basis of whether or not they can win the business. I've done this myself, walked away from deals where I may potentially be the best qualified provider simply because the odds of winning are so slim.

Now think about this from your perspective – you have identified a pool of the best possible providers, and the top two or three decide not to respond to your RFP. It only adds cost and time to their bottom lines and may yield no return. We all have to make decisions on how best to use our time and that may happen at your expense.

There are times when an RFP may not be the right path and can actually do more harm than good. So, when warranted, consider a different approach to addressing the need. This may include inviting potential providers to the table to have a discussion, followed by discovery sessions where everyone involved has the opportunity to fully understand the need and develop a solution that works. Then, solicit proposals outside of an RFP.

Here are some of the benefits to moving forward without an RFP:

- Inclusion of the best potential providers.
- Quicker entrance to implementing the optimal solution.
- Earlier return on investment and cost benefit.
- Reduced burden on your associates.
- Cost elimination of issuing an RFP.
- Reduced costs from potential providers.

When you know the optimal solution and partner, or potential providers will not participate in an RFP, consider a different direction. It very well may be beneficial for your company and the provider community to focus directly on identifying the need, developing a solution, and landing on the provider. That way, you can move more quickly through a negotiation and into implementation.

# Will a Potential Provider Respond?

Sometimes, an RFP is the right approach. But, as with an RFI, there are certain rules I follow in determining whether or not I will respond. Keep in mind that not every sourced solution begins with an RFI. Many will go straight to an RFP. So, here are the rules I follow when deciding whether or not to respond:

1.  **Have I met the decision maker?** This is generally not the sourcing executive; but, the business owner or sponsor of the initiative.

2.  **Is there an opportunity early in the process to meet with the business team and discuss the current state situation** (at a high level) **so that I understand if we can put together a solution that will be of interest?**

3.  **Do I have a relationship with the decision maker** (or team), **or can I build one that will influence the decision?**

4.  **Is my company the incumbent provider?** If I am the incumbent, and want to keep the business, I am going to respond. If the current contract has been a bad experience, then a decline-to-respond may be used as a means to exit the relationship.

5.  **Is this a pricing exercise?** Some will use an RFP process to test the marketplace and determine if the current provider is overcharging them. As soon as I learn this is the focus of an RFP, I am out. While some potential providers are price driven, many do not offer price as their primary benefit.

6.  **Do I genuinely have the ability to provide the right solution?** This is a tough one for new or young sales executives. Many are so hungry for a win they will chase deals that are not winnable – inclusive of responding to RFPs where there isn't a good solution or fit available from the potential provider.

7.  **Is there an opportunity to provide a recommended or alternative approach?** If a provider is restricted to answering a series of questions and completing pricing grids, without an opportunity to share a different approach, you are limiting the potential solution. This is a game changer. This one question will often tilt my interest in pursuing an opportunity. Companies who invite me to share my optimal approach move right to the top of the list.

8.  **Is the company truly prepared to make a decision to implement the recommended solution?** When customers ask who I compete against, I honestly answer that the single largest competitor I face is "status quo." A no-decision ranks

as the single largest reason I do not win opportunities to which I submit proposals. This can be a tough criterion, as it is not always obvious up front whether a decision to implement a solution will ever be made.

9. **Can I win?** Perhaps this should have been the first criterion I listed. It clearly is one of the most important. Successful sales executives are laser focused on winning deals. This doesn't mean we haven't all chased more lost opportunities than we care to admit. But, time well spent uncovering the ability to win can keep a sales executive working on what matters most. None of us are paid on the number of RFPs we respond to ... only the opportunities we win. If I don't think there is a much better than 50% chance of winning, I likely will not continue.

Some of the most frustrating RFPs are the ones that are pricing exercises to test the current provider's charges. There are ways to test your current provider without having to put other providers through the time and expense of an RFP. This does not even address the time and expense on your side. Since I only participate in opportunities that I may win, I will shy away from pricing exercises as soon as I see that this is the reason for the RFP.

For instance, when a brokerage firm decided to test their incumbent through a mini RFP, they claimed they were looking for a new partner. We prepared a number of pricing models and approaches to address the program requirements and things seemed to be progressing well. I was surprised when on our last conference call the customer told us the incumbent had a lower pricing model, as we were told they were looking for a new provider. When I brought up the early feedback that the incumbent would not be continuing with the work, the customer admitted this might not be the case and asked me to lower my prices. I immediately recognized the beginning of a pricing war, and for me, a no-win situation. If I won the business, it would be at margins that were barely acceptable for my company. A worst case scenario was the customer would use my pricing to continue beating down the incumbent until they arrived at a mutually agreeable structure ... and ultimately re-award them the business. Neither scenario seemed inviting enough for me to continue. I quickly thanked them for their time, and disengaged myself from the process.

After the call ended, the executive over the initiative phoned me to discuss my withdrawal and I politely explained how continuing to work on this particular initiative would be futile for both of us. I took the opportunity to assure him that my company highly valued our existing relationship and that this decision would not impact our interest in pursuing other opportunities with the firm. As you might imagine, delivery of a withdrawal message can be critically important. The executive understood our position, and appreciated my approach. While it was no surprise they chose to stay with the incumbent, we maintained an excellent business relationship and pursued many other opportunities together.

In the RFP process, it is fairly common to have multiple rounds where potential partners are eliminated before a final decision is made. Invariably, I will receive a message from the strategic sourcing executive offering congratulations for having made it to the "next round." I have to admit; this doesn't make me feel that great. Unless you plan on selecting multiple vendors, advancing to a next round or coming in second is not overly rewarding. Sadly, I have never been paid for coming in second when the decision is to single source.

One of the brightest strategic sourcing executives I know is Phil Hertz. A Dartmouth graduate, Phil is a former partner with the consulting firm Opera Solutions and has spent most of his career either running sourcing organizations or consulting in the sourcing space. He has a very unique approach to strategic sourcing. Phil once told me his job was to find, create and maintain a feeding frenzy of qualified potential providers. It didn't matter the scope of the initiative – his philosophy was always the same.

To create this feeding frenzy, Phil frequently met with and openly discussed details of a project's scope with various potential providers. If he didn't know the answers to questions asked by potential providers, he would go find them. If he was asked to meet with various stakeholders or project sponsors, he would arrange the meetings. Outside of restricted areas of conversation, usually protected by Non-Disclosure Agreements (NDAs) with current providers, nothing was off the table.

Phil's belief is that in order to keep potential providers interested, he has to share as much information as possible. Doing so only encourages their continued involvement. And, it will also benefit the organization looking to address the need. For him, a disappointing outcome is if one, or more, of the most capable potential providers withdraw from the opportunity because the process is too restrictive.

Some might think this approach can create an unfair advantage (or disadvantage, as the case may be). But, if you approach every opportunity as if nothing is off the table, and give each potential partner the same access, you have provided a very evenly matched playing field. In fact, those who engage and ask the right questions will likely bubble up to the top of your list for continued consideration. It can be a bit of an early review process in evaluating potential providers.

It is worth mentioning that while fairness is important – in some industries more so than others, the end-game is to find the absolute best solution for the identified need. I frequently see opportunities where the vetting process overwhelms the optimal solution for the company issuing the RFP and those responding. While structure is important, don't let the process overtake the situation so that you miss out on the best possible strategy.

## The Rules of the RFP

When an RFP is the right direction for your initiative, there are some basic rules that should be adhered to. These include explaining the process, anticipated deadlines, and who the competitors are.

By the time you reach the point of creating an RFP, you need to know the process you will use during the RFP response period, and once the proposals are received. Subsequently, this should be well documented in the RFP. Include the selection criteria you will use to evaluate the proposals and select a go-forward partner.

# The Competition

One of the pieces of information almost always missing from RFPs is a list of the invited potential providers. In each case I will ask the strategic sourcing executive for this list. Most are as surprised that I am asking for it as I am that it wasn't included to begin with. Not knowing who you are competing against is like showing up to a baseball game and the opposing teams having no idea who they are playing. How often has that happened? What is the harm of knowing? Is there a risk?

You may ask, "What's the benefit?" Knowing accomplishes a couple of things. First, as a potential provider, I will review the list of competitors to determine if I am in the right game or maybe even the right league. If there is commonality and solution strength among the core group I don't have, that may be a good signal to me I am not the right potential provider. The opposite may also be true. But, this helps know the level of understanding the strategic sourcing team has of the playing field.

Another benefit of knowing the competitors is it allows everyone to better interpret the current state and need. Generally, once I see the list of competitors, particularly if there has been a challenge in effectively communicating the need, I know we can fill in the gaps. Most sales executives intimately know their competitors along with the types of solutions they have available in the market. In the end, this will help the potential providers deliver a proposal that will more accurately address your need.

# Question and Answer Period in an RFP

Soliciting clarifying questions from the potential providers prior to the proposal due date is a reasonable and typical part of the process. It can help them to better understand the current state and develop the best recommended solution.

That said, a savvy sales executive will know that too many questions can lead to learning more information than is necessary. Outside of the obvious, clarifying questions can result in a couple of outcomes:

1. It provides feedback to the sourcing team of how well the potential provider understands the identified need, and can address it. As I consistently share with my team, you can ask stupid questions.

2. The answer to specific questions may narrow the recommended solution more than if the question had never been asked. This can be limiting for both parties. An RFP should be used to gather as much information as possible about the potential provider – and their recommended solution; not necessarily build the final deliverable.

For these reasons, I generally do not ask questions unless we cannot otherwise respond to a request or section of an RFP. However, I would never risk presenting a proposal where we do not have a complete grasp on the need and if questions are necessary, I will not hesitate to ask them. But, before that occurs, I have a rigorous internal review process to ensure any questions from my team are absolutely necessary. More often than not posed questions aren't passed on to the customer.

# Electronic Bidding Tools

A few years ago electronic bidding tools became quite popular. These can generally be broken down into a couple of categories: Electronic RFI / RFP tools, and reverse auctions.

## Electronic RFI / RFP Tools

Using an electronic procurement tool for collecting information can be a positive experience for the company sourcing a need and the responding providers. Generally, these tools are web-based and provide a very consistent means of reviewing the RFP contents and building / submitting responses. Of the tools I have used, Ariba® is the best. Acquired by the German software giant SAP® in 2012, Ariba is also one of the most expensive for companies to purchase and maintain.

Its intuitive nature and ease of use is what makes Ariba so attractive. Documents can be downloaded in an Excel format, allowing responders to answer questions or requests in the spreadsheet, and then re-uploaded. In addition, Ariba has excellent help tools, and in many cases a help-line you can call for assistance. Since many sourcing initiatives are timed events, being able to quickly resolve technical issues is a critical component. Finally, since so many companies use this toolset, there is a familiarity that makes for easy navigation. And, although customers can personalize their sites, there remains a relative constant with Ariba allowing it to be a comfortable experience for potential providers.

Some electronic tools limit the provider's ability to freely create a story or optimal format. While strategic sourcing executives may see this as a positive, potential providers will likely view it as a limiting factor. Since most sales executives will want to share an optimal alternative strategy, it is important to find a way that encourages and incorporates this into the process. As mentioned before, the objective of the entire process is to find the best possible solution to fulfill a need. Anything that is viewed as limiting, and potentially in place only to create a unified bidding process, can cause you to miss out on the best recommendation.

## Reverse Auction

For highly commoditized and mature products, a reverse auction may be used to find the lowest price available. The process is actually very simple – specifications are provided to potential providers prior to the auction. Then, on auction day, providers bid on the product. Once an opening bid is established, responders can lower their bids as they see others responding. This continues until no more bids are placed – which signals that the lowest bid has been received.

While this may work well for commodities, it has little use when value added services are involved.

The first time I was involved in a reverse auction was when a global overnight / small package shipping company decided to use this system for air bills and shipping labels that we were currently providing. Although the shipping company viewed these as commodities, they were actually highly customized and required a number of additional services, such as unique air bill numbering, personalization, custom packaging, and storage and distribution. We viewed this as a strategic solution. But, the products still went to auction.

A number of bidders were brought in to respond based on the provided specifications, and the auction opened at 8:00 am on a Friday. As one bidder would lower their price, all players had the opportunity to respond by lowering their bids. This went on until the last bid was submitted.

After a short time, the bids dropped below our costs and we stopped bidding. The head of our strategic accounts group, who was working with me on the auction, made the comment that this was the worst day of his sales career. Not because of the process that drove responses below our costs – but because he knew the competing providers had no real understanding of the full business requirements.

Not surprisingly, we were informed the following week that we lost the auction and as a result most of our business was moved to the low bidder. After a couple of months, we received a call from the client advising us that the low bidder could not produce the product at the price levels that won them the auction. And, they wanted us to re-engage as their primary supplier. We agreed, and renegotiated our contract.

Although this ended well, it was not a good experience for anyone involved. But, a valuable lesson was learned – when a product or solution is viewed as strategic by the sourcing team or the sales executive, a reverse auction is not the right approach. Since the majority of the programs I work on are strategic, I no longer participate in reverse auctions.

While electronic biding tools have their place in sourcing, don't let this be the deciding factor on how you source a required need. Even if your company has an electronic tool, let the need and potential providers direct you on whether it makes sense to use it. There may be occasions when a more traditional process will yield better results.

# Will I Play Again?

Every sales executive has delivered proposals they believe should have been the winning solution, but weren't selected.  And, there are those where they regret wasting their time.

Jeff Teal, a business development executive on my team, is one of the most successful sales executives with whom I have ever worked.  He is extremely creative in the development of solutions, and has the ability to quickly identify whether or not we can meet a customer's need. And, his tenacity and perseverance are unmatched. He is by far one of the most positive individuals I know, and even describes himself as an optimist.  Jeff frequently reminds me that lost RFPs are great learning experiences.  In these situations, we get to know a customer and a need we may otherwise not have seen.  In spite of some of the work yielding a less than desirable outcome, he is right.  And, this helps make us better at what we do.

Regardless of the outcome (win or lose), I always ask for a review or post mortem with the customer.  When we win, but even more so when we lose, it forces us to modify our solutions, and in many cases develop new ones. Fortunately, most customers are willing to provide this post-review feedback.

Be open and honest about who you chose and why.  The more in-depth feedback you provide a sales executive, win or lose, the better it is in the long run for the marketplace, your industry and your company.  It is not necessary to share information protected by NDAs – but sharing as much as possible helps everyone grow and become better.  Not sharing risks the potential provider from wanting to participate in the future with your company.

In an RFP for a small regional bank, an outside sourcing consultant had been retained to manage the process.  After meeting my initial requirements, we responded to the RFP – with what I thought was one of our best proposals.  I believed then, and still do today, that we had a solution that matched up perfectly to their need.  When we were not selected, I requested a review meeting but, the consultant declined.  He said he had never seen value in reviewing a decision with a provider that was not selected. He may be right but, neither of us will ever know. I have never worked with him again.

# Things to Stay Away from in an RFP

I could probably write an entire book on this topic. There are certain key elements that add little value to reviewing an RFP. If in doubt about whether a certain topic should be included, ask yourself one simple question, "Will the answer add any material value in the evaluation of the proposed solution?"

A few items you should stay away from:

1.  **In terms of overall spend, where would we rank among your customers? Please list your top five customers.**

    For confidentiality reasons, I would never answer either of these questions but, frequently see both. At the very minimum, this suggests that I might provide preferential treatment to customers based on size. The fact is most providers did not build themselves into a reputable company by giving more attention to customers based on revenue classification. Want to check me on this? Ask your own sales and operations departments how size of a company influences levels of service.

    In my own case, we built our business on fulfilling clients' needs and providing superior customer service. All of our customers are equally important and we do not have a business model that caters to customers based on size. Besides, would you really want to work with someone who did?

    The real interest is in knowing that when a problem occurs there is a process and escalation protocol to resolve the issue. Why not just ask this question?

I have found that providers who have lean organizational structures perform better in addressing this concern. A lean structure means there is a short path to get from the account management team to a senior executive who has the ultimate authority to fix a problem. By contrast a hierarchal organizational structure, where there are several layers of management, often makes it difficult to navigate to the few individuals who can really pull the trigger on addressing a problem or changing a business process.

2.  **Should your company be selected are there any legal proceedings which may prevent you from working with our organization?**

    If there are legal proceedings that may impact our ability to do business together, I will withdraw and I think any other sales executive will do the same. However, if you are that concerned, you may want to perform your own investigation.

    My typical response to this question is:

    *"There are no legal proceedings that we believe will impact our ability to move forward with an agreement to do business together."*

3.  **How long does it take to implement?**

    My standard answer to this question is 90 days. Anything less is considered not believable. And, anything more is too long in the eyes of the customer. The reality is I don't know how long it takes. Until I have built the complete solution, inclusive of a detailed project plan – and that you agree with, I will not know. Among other things, two key factors to determining how long an implementation takes are available time and resources from your company, and a fully built-out solution from the provider. At the beginning stages, rarely is either of these known so answers to this question cannot be counted on.

4.  **Please provide a detailed implementation plan.**

    Customized solutions generally do not come with an off-the-shelf project plan. In most cases the implementation will be highly customized to the solution. Even if the potential provider could cobble together a project plan template, why would they risk the potential of your company taking that and sharing it with another provider? Or, using it without selecting them? For this reason, I will not share a detailed project plan unless we are far along the path to being selected and I know it won't be used if I am not selected as the go-forward partner. Even then, it is rare I will respond to this request.

5. **Please have an authorized party sign the RFP indicating that if we move forward you will adhere to the information provided, including the pricing information.** This request must mean that at some time, potential providers submitted proposals that they later decided not to support in the contracting phase. Or, this verbiage was seen in someone else's RFP and the sourcing team thought it sounded like a great idea.

Most sales executives will stand by the offer once it goes to contract. But, there are two considerations worth thinking about. First, the optimal solution implemented will likely change as the process evolves. And second, the terms and conditions of the relationship will be negotiated as part of the contracting phase later in the process. These, too, will be based on mutual agreement with input from multiple sources (i.e. sourcing team, sales executive, attorneys, etc.).

While I respond to this request as presented, I do not feel it adds any material value to the process.

---

# Key Points

- Determine early in the process whether or not an RFP is right for you. Even if it is your company's policy to formally RFP a specific need, propose a different approach when you see it will better address the need.

- Will a potential provider respond to an RFP? Most sales executives will run through a series of questions they ask themselves to determine if moving forward makes sense for their company:
  - Have I met the decision maker?
  - Is there an opportunity early in the process to meet with the business team and discuss the current state situation?
  - Do I have a relationship with the decision maker, or can I build one that will influence the decision?
  - Is my company the incumbent?
  - Is this a pricing exercise?
  - Do I genuinely have the ability to provide the right solution?
  - Is there an opportunity to provide a recommended or alternative approach?
  - Is there a strong likelihood a decision to implement will be made?
  - Can I win?
- RFPs that are issued to "test the market," which usually means a pricing exercise, are often met with a "no-bid" from experienced sales executives. This is because these types of RFPs rarely yield a change in direction.
- When you decide that an RFP is the right approach for your initiative, you should adhere to basic professional rules that include explaining the process you will go through, anticipated deadlines, and who the competitors are.
- Savvy sales executives will pose very few questions during the Q&A period. Doing so can potentially box them in to a specific solution, or make them look less capable.
- In an RFP only ask questions that you develop and that will add value in helping you determine an optimal provider.

# 5

# CONTENTS OF AN EFFECTIVE RFP

The depth and content of an RFP may vary, depending on the nature of your need and the scope of the business requirements. But, there are key elements every RFP should contain. These elements should be tied to a logical path that will guide you and the potential providers from an identified need, through to the optimal solution and partner. Some of these may be obvious. Perhaps others are not.

## Figure 5.1 – Path from Identified Need to Optimal Solution and Partner

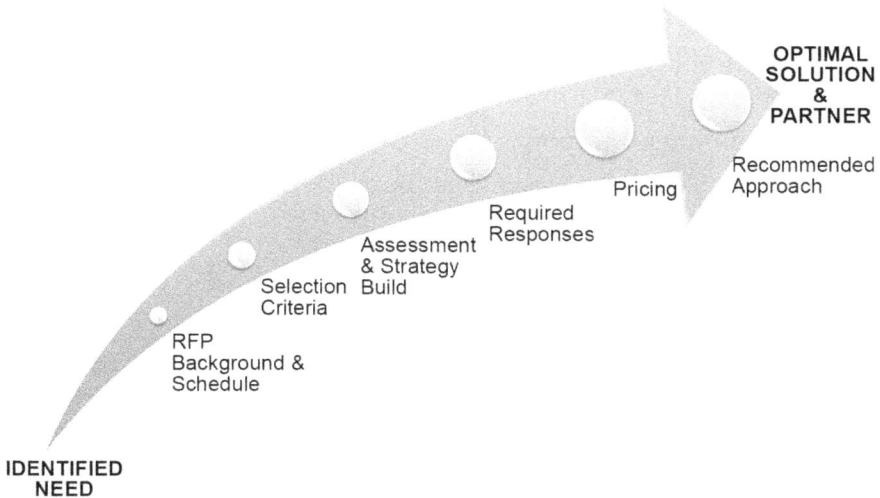

OPTIMAL
SOLUTION
&
PARTNER

Recommended Approach

Pricing

Required Responses

Assessment & Strategy Build

Selection Criteria

RFP Background & Schedule

IDENTIFIED NEED

1. RFP background and schedule
   a. Background of your company
   b. Description of initiative
      i. Current state situation
      ii. Need
      iii. Objectives
   c. Contacts during the RFP
   d. Schedule of activities
2. Selection criteria, including score sheet
3. Invitation to perform an Assessment and Strategy Build
4. Required responses
   a. Provider demographics
   b. Direct response questions
   c. Technology
   d. References
   e. Approach to implementation
   f. Subject matter experts / Bios
   g. Cost of solution
   h. Case studies
5. Pricing
6. Recommended approach / solution
7. Other available services (optional)

# RFP Background and Schedule

## Background of Your Company

This is one of the more critical elements in an RFP, and is often overlooked when preparing the document. If I had to guess, I would say that many are cut and pasted from previous RFPs, or other internal sources. And, little attention is given to how they will be received or used by the potential providers.

This is your opportunity to provide an in-depth explanation of your company, relative to the need. This means sharing information that cannot otherwise be found through other sources. It isn't about stating the need – but providing background on the company to support a better understanding of the need. For example, a company may have outgrown its ability to provide a certain service to its clients, and is looking to outsource. Explain in this section the growth of the company over the past few years. Provide insight into where your company has been, some of the current expectations and initiatives, and what the future might hold (within in legal limits, of course).

Resist the temptation to cut and paste from a previous RFP or the company website. Instead, create a story that fully explains the background of your company, relative to the need.

## Description of the Initiative

By far, the most important element of an RFP is a detailed description of the initiative. This includes the current state situation, synopsis of the need, and the objectives of the RFP. It is critical that the potential providers have every bit of insight possible that has driven you to source a solution in the market. Anything short of this will result in a potentially unusable proposal.

You may think that questions from the providers will later take care of any void here. But, actually quite the opposite is true. When the initiative is not clearly defined, questions posed from the potential providers will only broaden the gap. The reality is you cannot think of everything to put in an RFP – hence the need to offer and respond to questions from the potential providers. But, the more time you invest in clearly articulating the current state, identifying the need, and defining the RFP objectives, the better and more meaningful the responses will be.

To augment the description of the initiative, consider developing high-level workflow models that provide a visual of your current state.

This doesn't have to be a masterpiece of art, or even a detailed workflow drawing. It just needs to demonstrate how you currently get from point A to point B. Have the associates closest to the process assist with the description. If you have already tried various tactics to solve the need, mention that here. It will avoid receiving proposals containing what you already know doesn't work.

Since there will inevitably be gaps, strongly consider holding provider meetings early in the process. Plan on holding these sessions shortly after the RFP is issued but before any questions are posed. Depending on the situation, these sessions may be held jointly among all participating providers. Or, you may find it more advantageous to have individual meetings. Regardless, these sessions will go a long way to ensuring the providers fully understand your current state situation and the need you are trying to solve.

And, finally, share the project budget. I believe I just heard some audible gasps! But, think about it. If you are asking a potential provider to develop a solution, doesn't it make sense to share how much money you have to spend? I suspect most sales executives have developed really great solutions that are not affordable – only to learn this well after a significant amount of work has gone into developing the final proposal. The budget does not have to be exact – rather a ballpark. Perhaps it is aligned with what you spend today on a solution you have, but want to change. Or, it can be a "no more than X dollars…" discussion. Providing an estimated project budget will ensure you receive a proposal you can actually buy, as opposed to a really great one you cannot.

You may be asking yourself, "What if I don't yet have a project budget, and have no idea how to build one?" You will have these scenarios. When this occurs, engage your potential providers to help you build a couple of rough-cut scenarios and budget options. This is a good exercise to include in the early process of finding potential providers. Regardless, with enough input, even at a high-level, you can develop a budget range that should be shared with all of the potential providers.

## Contacts During the RFP

It is important to include a minimum of two contacts with your RFP, and multiple methods of reaching them. Most RFPs I see generally contain only one contact. And, invariably that is the one person in the organization that is next to impossible to reach. For that reason, having at least two contacts is highly recommended. Consider the downside – if a potential provider cannot reach key personnel for critical conversations, time is wasted and the proposal will suffer.

One of the more challenging elements for the potential providers is the restriction of access to the individuals who understand the current state and need better than anyone else. In fact, there are occasions when specific, and threatening, language is included on this topic, generally under the guise of ethical business practices. One such entry from an actual RFP:

> *"Please refrain from discussing this RFP with internal XYZ Corporation's staff other than the contact listed in this RFP. Doing so will be grounds for dismissal for continuation in the process at XYZ Corporation's sole discretion."*

There is nothing about the strong language here that makes sense. First, for reasons discussed earlier, having access to multiple subject matter experts will only help offer a better proposal. And, second, if I am offering up my free services to provide you with a proposal, I should not be verbally assaulted in the process.

In order to keep some level of control, it makes sense to have a clear chain of communication, so that everyone involved in the RFP is aware of conversations that are being held. It is even more important that critical team members of the sourcing initiative are kept abreast of conversations. But, consider using this as a means of managing access to the associates who have the knowledge of the current state situation. Encourage dialog with and participation from the individuals who can provide the most information to the potential providers. Keeping these individuals, and the project sponsor, engaged with the potential providers will help ensure you get the optimal solution and partner you are looking for.

Here is how the above example could have been reworded to have a more positive impact:

> *"Throughout the process, you may find it necessary to speak to one or more associates not listed as primary contacts for this RFP at XYZ Corporation. In the event you feel such contact will benefit your company in building an optimal solution, please call or email the contact listed in the RFP. We will make every effort to accommodate your request."*

It is important to note that ethical business practices are very important with every sourcing initiative – on both sides of the table. Hold yourself and the potential providers to the same rigorous standards, and choose to work only with companies who value business ethics as much as you do. However, if as in the case of the above example there is only one contact, provide some assurance to the potential providers they will have access to those who fully understand the business requirements and can answer specific questions. Equally as important, the named contacts have to be responsive.

## Schedule of Activities

Every RFP should have a targeted schedule of events or activities. This is the timeline of what will occur from the point an RFP is issued until a decision is made. It provides the expectation of what will occur during the process. Following is an example of a schedule of activities. Keeping in mind that your schedule may look different, a simple list of activities along with expected due dates is exactly what the potential providers are looking for.

From the sales executive's point of view, the schedule of activities is a critical piece of information. And, it should be in your organization, too. The schedule of activities should be taken very seriously. Give thought to what it will take in your company to make a decision – and all of the steps in between that will lead to the selection of an optimal solution and partner. Then, develop a timeline that you can reasonably adhere to. Circumstances may arise that interfere with the anticipated schedule of activities. When this occurs, communicate to the invited participants what is happening, what caused the change in schedule, and the anticipated or revised timeline. Be respectful of the time, effort and expense the potential providers are investing in preparing the requested proposal. And, recognize that in most cases only the provider that is awarded the business will recoup their investment.

**Figure 5.2 – Schedule of Activities Example**

| Activity | Due Date |
|---|---|
| 1. RFP Issued | Day 1 |
| 2. Meeting with Providers | Days 8 & 9 |
| 3. Clarifying Questions Submitted | Day 11 |
| 4. Clarifying Questions Answered | Day 17 |
| 5. Assessment & Strategy Build On-Site Sessions | Day 22 thru Day 26 |
| 6. Proposals Submitted | Day 47 |
| 7. Review of Proposals | Day 50 thru Day 54 |
| 8. Formal Presentations & Discussion with Selected Providers | Days 57 & 58 |
| 9. Internal Review, Selection and Notification of Award | Day 67 |
| 10. Contract Negotiation | Day 70 thru Day 95 |
| 11. Implementation Kickoff | Day 98 |

If you consistently move your own dates, while holding firm on the potential providers' deadlines, they will begin to lose faith in your process, including your ability to make a decision. Consistently missed deadlines by those issuing RFPs is a key indicator problems exist with the initiative. The impact to you could be as dramatic as one or more of the providers deciding to drop out of the process.

As a frequent responder to RFPs, I have found there is little flexibility on the deadlines to respond or present proposals. Some are so rigid, they provide a deadline date and specific time of day by which responses have to be submitted. Occasionally an extension will be granted – particularly if the majority of the invited participants are requesting one, or if the discovery period has yielded far more issues than anticipated. Regardless of the reason, give strong consideration when a potential provider asks for more time. There may be companies who will ask for more time simply because they procrastinated. But, for many the request is because they want to present you with the absolute best possible proposal. Keep in mind the objective of an RFP is to find the best solution and partner to solve a need.

Deadlines for presenting a proposal can sometimes get in the way of selecting the right solution or partner. While a deadline can be important, this is not a reasonable criterion for selecting the right solution or partner. Adhering to a process that potentially eliminates the best possible outcome isn't beneficial to you or the providers.

Early in my career I responded to an RFP for a regional financial services firm. It was issued by a strategic sourcing executive I had previously worked with when she was at another company. She knew we were capable of meeting the exact needs – as they were very similar to what she had experienced with us in her previous role. Because of this, I believed we had a very well aligned solution match. It didn't hurt that we had a great professional relationship.

I accidently entered the wrong due date in my calendar for the requested proposal. It was simply a clerical error on my part. Or, as my boss said, "You screwed up!" The afternoon it was due, at precisely 5:01 pm, I received a call from the strategic sourcing executive. She disappointingly advised me the RFP was due at 5:00 pm. In a moment of panic, I looked at my calendar and realized I had the due date logged as the following day. But, after reviewing the RFP's schedule of activities, I knew I was wrong.

The most frustrating part of this story is that I was finished with the proposal. But, I had to drop off a hard copy – which I had planned for the next day; what I thought was the actual due date. I told her I would immediately bring it over. She advised that she would not be there – as she was heading out for the day, but to leave it with the front desk.

She then went on to say that she doubted her company would accept it because the submission deadline was a key criterion.

I delivered the proposal, and as advised, the company rejected it. In fact, I was later informed they never read it.

That was a tough lesson – and one that has stuck with me ever since. Believe me; I have never missed another proposal deadline. But, to this day I often wonder if we had the best solution and they never knew.

# Selection Criteria

With every RFP, I ask for the selection criteria as well as the score sheet that will be used to evaluate the proposals and potential partners.

The selection criteria are different than the objectives of the RFP, which should be documented as part of the description of the initiative.

While most RFPs contain high-level selection criteria, very few include a score sheet. And, many companies will not provide one when asked. Some do not even have a formal process for evaluating proposals. For that reason, I have included a sample of what a high-level score sheet should look like.

Figure 5.3 – High-Level RFP Score Sheet

| Selection Criteria | Provider 1 | Provider 2 | Provider 3 | Provider 4 |
|---|---|---|---|---|
| **1. Financial Impact:** A total financial impact approach will be used in evaluating all responses. It is our objective to reduce its overall service / product costs and enhance revenue. | | | | |

| Selection Criteria | Provider 1 | Provider 2 | Provider 3 | Provider 4 |
|---|---|---|---|---|
| **2. Supplier's Capabilities:** Supplier's ability to meet the company's requirements and provide project implementation detail and timelines. | | | | |
| **3. Management Commitment:** Evaluated in terms of the quality and completeness of the Provider's response to the RFP and willingness to comply with the Terms and Conditions outlined in the RFP. | | | | |
| **4. Flexibility of Business Arrangements:** Provider's willingness to propose terms appropriate to the dynamic and competitive environment in which the company operates. | | | | |
| **5. Work Approach:** Covers the completeness of the services proposed, the willingness to satisfy RFP requirements, the quality of management, and the approach used to ensure high quality service. | | | | |
| **6. Negotiations Approach:** Relates to Provider's willingness to advance concrete proposals in this RFP response, and the completion of negotiations in accordance with the company's schedule. | | | | |

| Selection Criteria | Provider 1 | Provider 2 | Provider 3 | Provider 4 |
|---|---|---|---|---|
| **7. Staff Qualifications and Service Continuity:** Provider's commitment to employing an appropriate number of qualified professionals to ensure service continuity and problem resolution. | | | | |
| **8. Provider's strategy with respect to the RFP objectives:** Provider's ability to describe the optimal approach that will meet the company's overall objectives and result in cost savings. | | | | |
| <u>Average Overall Rating  ==></u> | | | | |

**Key:**

5 - Strong ability to exceed requirement with demonstrated / proven success

4 - Ability to exceed requirement

3 - Adequately able to meet requirement

2 - Partially meets, but generally lacks capability/willingness to fully meet

1 - Completely lacks capability / willingness of requirement

This score sheet is from an actual RFP; it was developed to be used by the sourcing team while evaluating the proposals. And, it was provided to all of the potential providers invited to participate in the RFP. From a sales executive's perspective, it was a refreshing change to see this included in the RFP.

As you review the sample score sheet, you will see there are only eight categories, and a simple scoring key. This is intentional. You may look at the contents of the eight categories, or maybe the sequence, and question the relevance of some of the entries. Used in your environment, some of these may not be relevant. The point is not the content, but the structure of the score sheet. Having a manageable number of categories will help those using the tool (on both sides of the table) to understand what you are looking for and what matters most. The more complex a scoring sheet becomes, the less effective it is in ranking of the potential providers. How many times have you used a score sheet, only to discover at the conclusion that the ranking of the providers is not remotely close to how you really feel? This is likely due to the complexity. So, keep it simple, but relevant.

The scoring key should also be easy to understand and manage. The wider the range of scoring choices, the more ambiguous the results will be. Some of my colleagues argue the scoring system should be limited to a scale of 1 to 3. Only you will know the right approach. But, I think 1 to 5 is a great range to consider.

# Assessment and Strategy Build

Consider inviting the potential providers to perform a current state assessment in order to build the optimal solution. It can be the difference between getting the right solution for your need and receiving a number of proposals that provide no value.

As much as you believe the RFP contains the most well-thought-out and complete description of the need, you will never effectively cover it in the eyes of any potential provider. They are subject matter experts trained to define, at a deep level, your current business operations and solution requirements.

Think about the natural progression of understanding the current state in order to build a solution that addresses the need, before you are ready to make a decision and launch. A three-phased process, or stair step, is a logical approach, and starting with a current state assessment of the operation is a good idea. This feeds into developing the best-fit solution in the solution design phase. Then, in the final step, the optimal partner will implement the solution and track its success.

## Figure 5.4 – Assessment and Strategy Build Process

Financial
Benefit

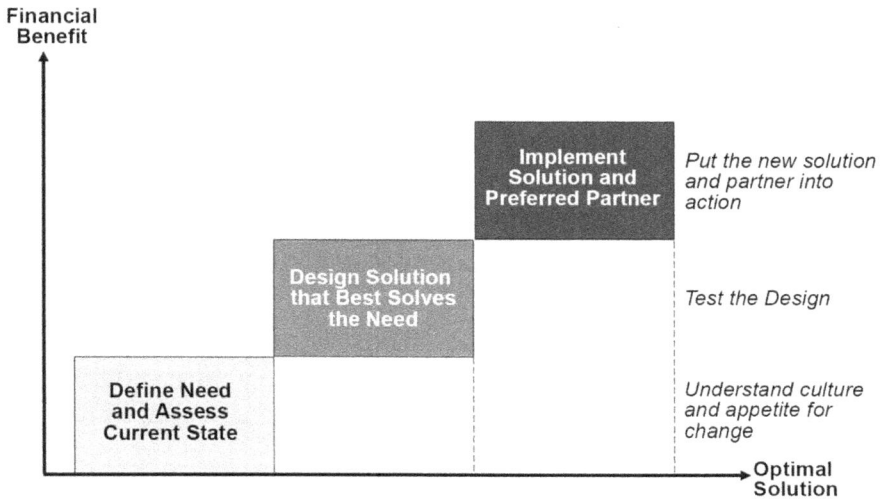

| | |
|---|---|
| **Implement Solution and Preferred Partner** | *Put the new solution and partner into action* |
| **Design Solution that Best Solves the Need** | *Test the Design* |
| **Define Need and Assess Current State** | *Understand culture and appetite for change* |

Optimal
Solution

# Define Need and Assess Current State

Even though you may have done an excellent job defining the current state and need, there will always be additional information that will help the potential providers. This extends beyond the question and answer period in most RFPs. For this reason, a current state assessment should be included in your RFP process.

Depending on the need, the current state assessment is often best started on-site, and in person. The on-site part may be able to be completed in a couple of days, or less. And, depending on the scope and complexity of the initiative, the entire process may be completed in as little as 30 days. Regardless of the time it takes, give the potential providers the opportunity to gain a first-hand understanding of your business situation as it exists today. Provide access to the individuals who can answer questions and guide them through the current state process. And, allow the potential providers a chance to ask questions and interact with the line or lines of business. This should include the project sponsor, and the team that will be making the decision.

The current state assessment, when done correctly, will yield several valuable outcomes for both you and the potential provider:

## Your Company

1. Gives you a first-hand look at the subject matter expertise of the potential provider. The more of your team members who are involved, the better perspective you will have. The current state assessment, when deployed, should become an evaluation criterion.

2. Provides a chance to evaluate the cultural compatibility between the two organizations. At the point you select an optimal solution and provider, it is imperative you know you can actually work with them.

3. Allows your team to interact with the potential providers and ensure they fully understand your current state and identified need.

## Potential Provider

1. Allows them to understand your current operation, and identify any gaps not understood regarding the need.

2. Provides an opportunity to develop a workflow model of the current state that can visually help in building the right solution.

3. Gives their team an opportunity to interact with the organization and understand the culture. Culture is half the necessary information in order to build a solution that will work in your environment.

4. Allows them the opportunity to float ideas past your team for initial and immediate feedback.

In some cases, you may have contracted with an outside consultant who has already performed their own current state assessment. Or, you may have performed a similar study with internal resources. Although you or your consultant may be experts in identifying a problem – you have to rely on the potential providers to propose the recommended solution. And, since they are the subject matter experts, they need to perform their own assessment.

If work has been completed through your own efforts prior to or in preparation for an RFP, and you believe some of the current state assessment will be redundant, pass your findings on to the potential providers. They can use that information as a starting point. Try and refrain from withholding information from the potential providers you uncovered in your own assessment. And do not operate under the assumption that your assessment can replace what the potential providers will want and need. Since the objective of the RFP is to uncover the absolute best solution and optimal partner – now is not the time to hold back.

## Design Solution that Best Solves the Need

With the work performed in the current state assessment, the potential providers can begin to build the optimal solution. In fact, the solution build should begin taking form during the current state assessment.

It is important that your project team be part of the strategy build process. As potential solutions are developed by the providers, have them vet those with you and your team. This is like a trial balloon – to gauge reactions from the project team. The reason for doing this early in the process is it allows the potential providers to receive feedback on how the solution ideas are being received, and if they can possibly be ingested into the company as the optimal solution.

Two of the largest barriers to any solution being implemented are culture of the buying organization and the ability to execute. Some companies lack the appetite and discipline to implement change. Others may have never outsourced a significant need – and therefore do not have the experience. And, a number of companies are concerned about losing control if too much of a solution is outsourced beyond their own brick and mortar. The ability to execute is probably a larger issue than any of us give credit. I have heard, "The strategy was sound; we failed to execute," far too many times to count. However, if you can't or don't execute, whatever the reasons may be, the strategy is a failure. As you are vetting the potential solutions, you have to take honest stock as to whether you and the potential partners can actually pull off implementation. Regardless, both you and the provider community have to learn where those lines in the sand are – specifically understanding what will and will not work in the final solution design.

As ideas emerge, the provider community should continually float them by you and your team. The consistent review and presentation of ideas throughout the process has a couple of benefits:

1. **You will know the final solution before it's presented.** When done correctly, you will be able to provide feedback throughout the development phase and the final solution presented is one that you know and are comfortable will work in your organization.

2. **Potential providers will be able to develop and hone in on a solution they know will work in your environment.** No one in the provider community wants to invest time in creating a solution that cannot be implemented.

The challenge for you and your team during this process is to be honest about your current state, and to keep an open mind during the strategy development. Sometimes it's uncomfortable to show the severity of your current situation. But, if you are honest about where you are in the current state assessment, it will only help the solution development process. Ideas to help solve the need are directly dependent upon knowing everything there is to know about what happens today.

Similarly, the solution development can be a difficult process to fully embrace. As a sales executive, I know that any solution I bring to the table is going to invoke some level of change. Since most people are averse to change, it's a matter of understanding how much change a company can handle. When I first started selling high-end strategic solutions, I mentored with some of the best sales executives in the business. One executive, a vice president of business development, used to open sessions on solution development with the following phrase:

### *"Think about how it <u>could</u> be, not how it is today."*

Easier said than done. But, keeping an open mind on the potential options may be the difference in truly solving the issue and placing a Band-Aid on it. Besides, a well-qualified partner will have the experience to help you through the rough patches of changing your business approach.

One of the largest RFPs I ever participated in was for a company that administered financial retirement programs, primarily 401k plans. Up to this point, they internally prepared, mailed and/or pushed electronic statements and other communications to their corporate plan holders and individual account owners. As their organization grew, the demand for communication options was shifting, and the continued investment of managing this internally had become unattractive. So, they looked to the external provider community to help solve the need – with potentially outsourcing their entire distribution of communications. Since they had never done this before, we termed them a "first-time outsourcer." A first-time outsourcer is often looking for a solution they are unfamiliar with. As a result, the process is frequently a bit unorganized, if not completely wobbly. But, this company had one of the best and well thought out approaches I have ever seen.

During the on-site current state assessment, we began floating potential solution ideas by the project team. Some of the ideas were a bit outlandish, while others were somewhat conservative. This helped us better understand what would work in their organization, and what would not. Not only was the project team available throughout the on-site assessment, they were eager to engage with my team and discuss potential solution ideas. And, they kept an open mind about each solution alternative presented. They would often ask themselves, "Well, why not?" which forced a fair evaluation of why a potential solution may not work as opposed to just saying "no." It is important to note that the access was far reaching – and included the entire project team.

Representatives from sourcing, various lines of business, technology, human resources, finance and the project executive sponsors were equally engaged in the on-site meetings.

Prior to submitting our final proposal, the customer offered to have a pre-meeting with us to review the write-up. We prepared a written document and formal presentation, as I normally would. But, the customer had the opportunity to see a sneak-peek of the documents. This was presented via e-mail, and followed up with an in-person round table discussion. The two things that came out of it were identical to the anticipated outcomes identified earlier in this chapter:

1. The customer already knew the solution we were going to present because it had been vetted throughout the solution build process, with frequent feedback.
2. We received recommendations on how to tweak the proposal so that it fully met the customer's need which allowed us to go back and make final edits before presenting.

This collaborative, engaged process made all the difference in the proposal. Even before we said a word in the formal presentation, the customer knew the solution would meet their needs. And, we knew it was completely aligned with the project team's expectations.

## Implement Solution and Preferred Partner

There may be times when the selected provider will be the architect of the solution; but, not necessarily the builder. However, in many cases the solution architect of a need you source will be the best choice to build and implement the optimal design. In those cases, there can be a tight connection between the solution design and the implementation of the optimal strategy.

In addition, when the architect of the solution is the same as the source that will build and deliver it, the accountability goes up. It's easy to hold one company accountable in an implementation if it's the same one who designed the solution. For that reason, I much prefer to build and deliver the solutions we design. We have had scenarios where we only architect the strategy. But, actually building the end result allows us to ensure it will work once deployed.

# Required Responses

As a sales executive, I view this as the "ugh" part of an RFP. I understand it is a necessary part of the process; but it is a lot of work and doesn't allow me to tell my story or specifically address your need. Many times, the questions have little to do with whether or not you actually select me or my solution. That said, it is worth reviewing some recommendations to make this useful for you and at the same time palatable for the responding providers.

## Questions / Requests

When I first receive an RFP, and have gotten past the schedule of activities and rules of the process, I quickly move to the requests or questions that require specific responses. I am looking to determine if I can better understand the need, identify duplicate questions, and see how savvy the sourcing team is.

The questions asked will often provide additional insight into the need. As mentioned earlier, there will always be uncertainty on the part of the providers. These requests within the RFP may actually provide some of the missing links to uncovering the need, and save me from asking questions during the Q&A period.

From the sourcing team's side of the table, the questions have to be meaningful. This means that the responses should contribute to the sourcing team's goal of making a decision on the various offers. I often see questions in an RFP that I know were simply cut and pasted from another RFP with little thought to the relevance of the need at hand. If you plan to use the proposals to vet potential solutions that fit your need, it's worth taking the time to develop questions that will actually provide you with information to make a sound go-forward decision.

Frequently, I notice duplicity in questions. I have come to realize this is due to individual members of the sourcing team weighing in on what each wants to know, and their lack of ability to consolidate the questions. Specifically, I can tell that various internal business owners often create their own wish list of questions. These owners may include Information Technology (IT), the lines of business, operations, finance, manufacturing, etc. And, frequently they may have similar interests and questions.

When duplicate questions appear in an RFP, I answer each one as if I have never seen it before. However, I do cut and paste the same response in each duplicated place. As I do this, I often wonder how the answers are received by the company evaluating the responses. Is it as annoying to them as it is to me?

The solution to this is to have one individual aggregate the RFP questions, and ensure duplicate questions are eliminated. This requires the aggregator to be fairly familiar with the need and have a thorough understanding of what each contributor is trying to uncover. And, they need sufficient time in the process to perform this function. The objective here is to provide a fluid and concise RFP that is easy to follow, yet not overly invasive on the potential partners' time.

A savvy sourcing team will deliver an RFP with questions that are specific and to the point. They will avoid questions that add no material value – and limit their questions to those that truly benefit them in the selection process. Just as with questions asked from the potential providers, RFPs can also contain stupid questions. Don't underestimate the fact that the potential providers are evaluating your company based on the questions asked in the RFP. Succinct and well-thought out questions will go a long way to ensuring there is benefit to you and the potential providers.

## Careful What You Ask For

The goal of an RFP should be to identify the solution and partner you want to work with. This does not always mean identifying a completely built-out solution. Often that will come later. Since the questions are intended to help you make that ultimate decision, sensible and relevant questions are imperative.

In answering requests or questions in an RFP, I have a hard and fast rule: Answer the question, and no more. This includes requested pricing. Sometimes a sales executive can paint himself into a corner and open Pandora's box by providing information that was not asked in the question. Equally, the sourcing team may ask questions not necessarily related to the need, making the responses more difficult to evaluate. I see this more on RFPs where we are the incumbent, and the questions may refer to needs that I know don't really exist.

When this occurs, I answer the question very directly and to the point – even when I know it is irrelevant. The tendency for an incumbent is to use the knowledge they have to respond to the question. The problem with that is it throws off the fair evaluation of the proposals. For example, I may be asked about the cost structure to store product in one of my distribution centers. But, the question does not address picking, packing and shipping the product. If I add these cost elements to my answer, I am immediately viewed as having offered a higher priced solution. Whether relevant or not, I answer questions exactly as posed. Then, when you compare me to the other potential partners, I have a fair shot.

In some situations, the incumbent may want to talk to the souring executive and tell them they left out specific elements that may affect their ability to fairly evaluate the potential providers. When I am the incumbent and discover missing, incorrect or misleading information in an RFP, I will advise the client. Especially when I think it could impact the fair evaluation of the proposals. Then, if the client informs all of the respondents what I have shared (usually in the form of an updated RFP), I will respond accordingly. There are times when the client chooses not to update the RFP with insights I may have shared. Unless an update is provided to all participants, I will simply answer the questions in the RFP exactly as presented. I will only use my insights, particularly from a pricing standpoint, when the information is shared with the entire group participating in the RFP. Approaching this any differently will result in me providing a proposal that cannot effectively be compared to the other respondents.

The problem comes down to the final selection. When you ask questions that are not relevant or well thought out, you will have to address the gaps at some point with the selected partner. This can be uncomfortable for both parties.

Over the years I have had a lot of spirited conversations with my internal teams over how to answer questions or requests in an RFP. Many want to build the entire solution in the response. My goal is to respond to the questions, provide the right strategy to get to the optimal solution, and win the business. It is in neither of our best interests to provide you with a play-by-play on how to solve the need. As soon as I do that, I have lost any strategic value for which you may actually pay later on. And, you are holding a detailed solution that may not completely solve the need.

## Contract Review

A popular inclusion in many RFPs is a copy of the company's standard terms and conditions, often in the form of a Master Services Agreement (MSA), or contract. The request is for the potential providers to evaluate, or "redline" the contract. This is where the provider's business and legal teams will submit edits (with "track changes" turned on) so the company can see just how difficult the contracting process might be. The interesting part of this exercise is that it doesn't take into account the actual, agreed upon solution, which can influence the final agreement. So, to redline a contract in conjunction with the proposal seems a bit premature.

During an RFP for a manufacturing company, one of the requirements was to review the included MSA and return it with our redlined changes. This MSA was nearly 100 pages, most of which were a "boiler plate" language that would never pertain to our solution. As I scanned it, I could only think of the daunting process in front of me and the various stakeholders in my company to review it, even before our legal team took a crack at it.

Prior to beginning the internal review, I called the customer and asked the purpose behind it. His response was, "We want to see how much you guys 'bleed' all over the document. It is one of the selection criteria – the more red you have, the lower your score on that piece of the RFP." Well, that made it easy for me. We did not redline a single word in the MSA. Rather, we accepted it as written, but added the following statement:

> *"There is nothing in the MSA that would prevent our two companies from negotiating an agreement that will uphold the solution presented in our proposal. As part of the negotiation process, each of us may want to review specific language that pertains to the final agreed upon solution."*

I have since used similar language on most responses to RFPs requesting a review of an attached MSA. It's worth noting I have never lost a deal that has reached the point of negotiating a contract. When both companies want to do business, the contract becomes a formality, and most issues are overcome with a bit of give and take. Remember, it's about finding a solution and partner to address a need – not the process.

# Pricing

How many times have you received a proposal or response to an RFP and immediately flipped to the pricing section? As a sales executive, I have to admit I grumble just a bit when I see this happen. This is because it sends a message that the solution and potential ROI is not nearly as important as the price tag. I could have pitched a most ridiculous solution … but the only way I garnered any immediate attention was the price. A more logical approach is to first read and understand the contents of the proposal. Then after that, review the pricing.

As you think about evaluating the pricing of a solution, try to be open minded about how the solution is priced. Many RFPs I see include a market basket pricing exercise. This is a sampling of products and services where the potential providers deliver unit prices displayed in a spreadsheet or electronic tool. While this may be informative in some scenarios, it may also be limiting. Allow the potential providers to share an optimal pricing approach – along with numbers (dollars). In doing so, it is ok to challenge them on how they arrive at a cost structure so that you can learn if they fully understand your business. The worst that can happen is wrong assumptions are made and the final pricing is not reflective of what you or the selected provider thought.

One of the most unusual RFPs I responded to was for a major US-based airline. We were the incumbent, so responding to the RFP was not optional. The pricing section included a market basket of products and services the sourcing team believed to be relevant to our current program. As part of this, it contained only products and services that were easily ordered in increments. For example, a marketing brochure was included with three different quantity options. Technology was described, with an "ask" for the monthly subscription fee. As we reviewed the pricing request, we quickly realized there was no commonality between the program we currently managed and the RFP. The quantities were unrealistic and the technology described would not address their needs.

We approached the customer with our concerns that the pricing section may not accurately represent the program they currently had, or would want moving forward. On the surface the sourcing executive appeared interested, but later decided not to alter the RFP. He advised it would cause too much confusion to rework and distribute to the potential providers. And, that it would take more time than they had allotted in their process. So, he proceeded down the path of soliciting proposals that would not fulfill their needs – at least from a pricing perspective. The only difference between me and the other competitors is that I knew this was a bad approach.

The real reason for the lack of movement on this was the airline's desire to place all of the responses in a consolidated spreadsheet and compare the data. The more complex the solution, the more challenging it is to pop the numbers into a spreadsheet and compare one vendor to another. This is often what happens, though, in pricing exercises.

Customers give into the complexity of pricing a custom solution by using the easy way out – a simple spreadsheet that doesn't really address the need or the proposed solutions.

As a result of the customer's resistance to change the RFP, our pricing came in rather attractive – as we knew if the airline implemented our solution, this would not be the pricing used. So, the risk of responding with aggressive pricing was minimal. In the end, my company was selected as the continued provider. But, very little information provided in the pricing section was included in the final agreement. In fairness to the airline, we did offer an attractive pricing model that provided a best-in-class solution with a recognizable return on investment over the life of the agreement. Unfortunately, the market basket yielded no material benefit.

Occasionally I am asked for specific information on how my costs are derived – down to full disclosure on the gross margins I will make on the program. For competitive reasons, even if you have signed a non-disclosure agreement, know that most potential providers are not going to share this information with you. How we make money on sold programs should be of no concern to you. You are probably thinking that's a bit harsh. And, maybe it is – to a slight degree. But, there are certain pieces of information that each provider will believe is proprietary to their company and shouldn't be shared.

Consultants can be even more invasive with this request than customers who handle their own sourcing. I have been involved with some who want to understand specifics on how I will manufacture and the hourly cost of each work effort component. Unfortunately, this doesn't help the process. It is highly unlikely that understanding how I build, manufacture or price my solutions will change the quote.

I believe the real objective of the pricing section is to determine three things:

1. Is there a financial benefit to the recommended solution?
2. Is the solution affordable?
3. Is the offer competitively priced within the market?

Unless the need is so large that it outweighs any cost consideration, there should be a financial benefit. This benefit may be a return on investment, or a cost savings. And, it is necessary to know if the solution is affordable. Does it fit within the budget or can it pay for itself if implemented? Finally, is the recommended solution competitive in the marketplace? Weighing in on this specific question is how commoditized vs. customized the solution is. The more commoditized, the easier it is to determine if the solution is competitive. When a solution is customized, it may be difficult to determine market competitiveness. And, in these scenarios it may not even be relevant.

In any case, if the goal is to answer these three questions, serious consideration should be given to what you ask of the potential providers regarding the pricing. Specifically, the consideration should focus on how you plan to evaluate the responses.

The ideal scenario is to ask the potential provider for a cost analysis of their recommended solution. One of the best RFPs I responded to asked for a sample invoice for two billing cycles or periods. We were asked to provide two separate and detailed invoices for the months of January and February, respectively. The customer asked that we include everything we intended to invoice, exclusive of implementation and start-up costs – just as if the program were live and fully operational. Data used to support the invoice was gathered during the current state assessment of the opportunity.

This proved to be an eye-opening experience for me and the customer. After preparing the invoice, we both had questions. I made some assumptions because certain data I needed was not gathered or available during the assessment. And, the customer found certain invoice elements they had not expected. This provided an excellent platform to negotiate how an invoice would be constructed. And, it gave the customer an easy mechanism to answer the three questions above.

Unless the solution is highly commoditized, using a market basket – or sampling of products and services is ineffective in answering the questions. And, even then, it is often a snapshot in time, or may contain scenarios that are not completely representative of the actual business.

Essentially, a market basket or unit pricing exercise rarely provides a realistic view of what is going to happen after a contract is signed.

A sales executive with a global aircraft manufacturer once explained to me that companies can actually determine how effective their RFPs are by the pricing responses they receive. When the spread of financial offers is wide and varied, it is likely that the RFP was poorly written. This may mean specifications were vague or missing, or the need was not effectively defined. On the other hand, if the majority of the financial offers are reasonably aligned, the RFP was well-written.

Companies who fail to realize their financial objectives of RFPs often do so because of the requested pricing approach. This leads to disappointment, and sometimes finger pointing at various individuals with either the sourcing team or the sales team. In fact, I am convinced that some companies churn RFPs every three to five years because they have no other way of managing the results of RFPs that contain market basket pricing.

# Recommended Approach

As mentioned earlier, the ability to provide a recommended approach is a "must have" criterion for me to respond to an RFP. Although your RFP may be near perfect, the potential providers have a well-defined subject matter expertise in solving your need. As a result, you need to entertain a recommended approach in order for them to bring you the right solution. Anything short of providing this opportunity sends a message that you already know the solution, and you just want your questions answered along with the pricing grid filled out. Most strategic sales executives will not respond to this type of RFP.

When the recommended approach offer is missing from an RFP, I will usually contact the sourcing executive to ask if we can provide one. When the answer is no, I withdraw. But, those who are really interested in solving their need will welcome the recommended approach.

The recommended solution should be a free-format document allowing the potential providers to craft their approach in any manner they choose. As soon as the providers are boxed in, the creativity of their expertise becomes affected. Since this is a blank canvas approach, it's best to refrain from giving too much guidance. However, there are some key components that I think make for a good recommended approach:

- **Executive Summary** – This should be a two-page synopsis of the provider's recommended solution. The idea is that any senior executive in your company should be able to read the document and walk away with a good overview of the suggested approach.

- **Restate Current State** – The provider should indicate their understanding of the current state. This may be augmented with workflow models or information gleaned from any current state assessment discussions.

- **Recommended Approach** – This is a recap of the actual "how to" solve for the need. How does the provider take you from where you are today to solving the need? Included go-forward workflow models are a bonus in this section!

- **Cost** – What is the cost to get from where you are today to where you want to be? This may not be fully baked – and that's ok. If not, then it should address the pricing approach.

- **Implementation Approach** – How do you get the recommended approach off the ground? This may be a high-level timeline of the approach.

- **Subject Matter Expertise** – Who are the experts, along with their bios, that are going to build and implement the optimal solution? Explain why these are the right resources. The best way to do this is to connect the potential provider's subject matter experts back to the corresponding resources in your own company – and ensure they are a good fit.

- **Company Background** – Brief overview of the provider's company. What makes them unique in this space? What is it about their business that makes them believe they are best suited to solve your need?

Courtney Allen, a senior sales and marketing executive, has a keen sense of understanding what a customer is looking for in a proposal, and the most accurate assessment I have seen of the recommended approach document. He believes this is the place where the potential provider tells their story. Creating the proper environment and context allows the message to be understood exactly as they intend. In fact, Courtney views the recommended approach as the only part of the proposal that really differentiates one competitor from another. With other sections of the RFP, there is limited space or access to expand on how the provider would solve the need. The recommended solution is the chance to take the customer from the current state to the implemented solution – wrapped in a "story" that is relevant and easy to follow. While everyone will approach this differently, the story methodology resonates best, is easy to follow and understand, and can be a pivotal point in the process. As Courtney once told me, "It's not so much what you say as how you say it, that often matters most."

Don't pass up on this most critical step in soliciting proposals – whether through an RFP, or directly through conversations with the potential providers. It may feel a bit like "free-wheeling" but, you will find that a recommended approach may bring out a solution option you had not previously considered. Granted, reading and understanding the recommended approaches will take some time. And, it is not the kind of response that fits neatly into a spreadsheet. But, even with the extra reading, there is no risk. If you dig into an alternative approach and later decide it's not the path you want to go down, there's no harm done. And, if you find the best solution through a recommended approach, you are better off than you ever knew.

# Other Potential Services (optional)

I always enjoy and appreciate an opportunity to briefly present other potential services I think may interest the customer. Sometimes these services can directly impact or benefit the identified need. In other situations, it may have little to do with the RFP. From a few perspectives, extending a chance for the potential provider to share what else they have to offer can add value to your company.

1. There may be a chance to provide services in addition to solving your immediate need.

2. You might have another need for which you have been struggling to find a solution and, the additional services may be able to address it.

3. There could be a cost benefit to using both the solution being provided and the additional services – a "bundled" offering, if you will.

4. The additional services could help reduce the number of providers you are using. Since many companies strive to use fewer providers, this may be of importance.

5. Sometimes the additional services can change how you look at your specific need. I have seen situations where additional services, combined with the original offer, allows the customer to think more strategically about their need - and how to best address it.

I am sure you have encountered situations where you have said to a potential provider, "I didn't know you offered that service." As often as you may have said these words, rest assured there is a provider who is thinking, "I had no idea you needed that service."

Never pass up an opportunity to learn what else the provider community has to offer.

---

# Key Points

- There are key elements every RFP should contain. They should be tied to a logical path that will guide you and the potential providers from an identified need to the optimal solution and partner.

- RFP background and schedule
- Selection criteria
- Assessment strategy and build
- Required responses
- Pricing
- Recommended approach

- Invite potential providers to share other services they may be able to provide – even if they seem only loosely connected to the specific need you are sourcing.

# 6

# FINANCIAL BUSINESS CASE

K nowing if there is a financial business case for solving a need is a critical element for both you and the provider community. There are two levels of a financial business case: initial business case and cost benefit analysis. The first is a high-level determination of whether you should even invest in pursuing a solution and engaging potential partners. This is generally performed early in the process – such as during an RFI. The second is a financial deep dive into determining whether the optimal solution will provide the desired financial payback or cost benefit, if implemented. This is typically performed at the point of identifying one or two potential providers. When utilized, it often occurs in conjunction with the RFP process.

During one of my first meetings with Phil Hertz, an experienced consultant and sourcing executive, he told me that when solving any business need, data matters most. This means every need and potential solution has to be validated with data that supports moving away from the current state. It also requires that the proposed solution, or concept has data that supports moving forward. I took this to heart, and have since been using data driven business cases and financial analyses to support the solutions I recommend. In short, the best way to approach any financial business case is with data-rich, fact-based information.

## Initial Business Case

The initial business case is a quick analysis to determine if there is reason enough to continue pursuing a solution for a specific need. As a result, it needs to be performed early in the process. You are probably wondering how you do this if you don't know what you don't know. It's sort of like the chicken or the egg. But, there is likely sufficient information that you do know, or can uncover to potentially help you address your need.

The initial business case should be drafted as an editable document addressing five required questions, or components:

1. Can you define the need in a manner that will allow your organization to invest the time to effectively assess it and develop potential options?
2. What happens if you do not solve the problem?
3. What are the known potential options for solving the need?
4. Can your company provide enough dedicated resources to solve the problem – from conception through implementation?
5. Is there a strong likelihood of a return on investment or financial case to support moving forward?

**Figure 6.1 – 5 Parts of the Initial Business Case**

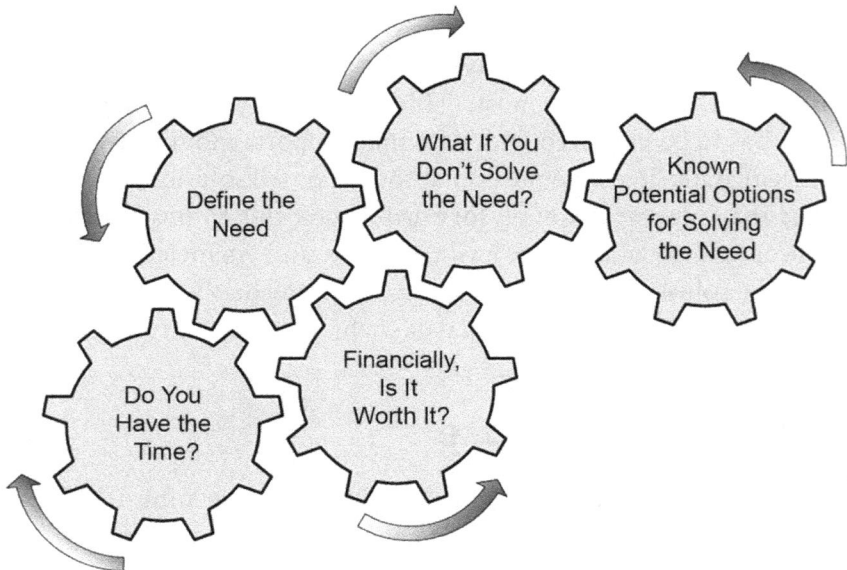

Each of these elements is interlocked with the others. One is not more important than any of the others. This means you need a favorable response to each component in order to keep the process moving forward. Ultimately, these five elements become the basis for the document addressing the initial business case.

## Define the Need

We have discussed the importance of defining the need in earlier chapters. But, it is equally important to make this an integral part of the initial business case. Your sourcing team and business sponsors have to be able to effectively articulate the need to the financial and executive community of your organization. They will likely be the influencers and decision makers of whether or not you move forward. As explained earlier, it is imperative to define the need in such a way that it can easily be understood, even by those not directly involved with the project. This includes stating any assumptions so there is full disclosure during the process. It may take some work, and vetting with internal resources to ensure you have it down right.

It is equally important to ensure the potential providers understand the definition of the need. In fact, it's worth floating your need by them to obtain their assessment of how you describe it. As you are putting an initial business case together it is critically important that how you define the need internally matches up with the provider community's understanding. Otherwise your internal teams and executives will think of the need differently than those who will ultimately be recommending solutions.

## What if You Don't Solve the Need?

A question my team constantly evaluates is, "What happens if a decision is never made to address the need and change from the current state? Does it matter?" From your perspective, and that of the potential partners, this needs to be addressed in the initial business case.

If not moving forward creates a critical failure in your business, then finding a solution is imperative. On the other hand, if there is no real impact to the business if you do nothing, the direction might be as simple as abandoning the initiative. Unfortunately, the decision line is not as simple as these two extremes. In most cases the answer to this question is somewhere in between.

Document the potential issues and outcomes if you invest in the initiative and decide not to move forward. There could be financial implications to the business, cost impacts regarding the current state, or risks to your business and customer base.

When you have a weak initial business case, or are struggling to gain internal support, raise the flag to your executives *and* the potential providers. In many cases both may be able to help you. If funding or resources is a problem – let the executives help guide you here. By contrast, if it appears there is a weak business case, ask the potential providers for guidance. Chances are they have seen this before, and have helped customers in very similar situations.

In the end, if all parties agree there is no material impact if you do not continue the project, then admit it's ok to abandon it – even if it means a bruised ego. Then, share this information with the potential providers. And, do it early in the game. Acknowledge that they are as busy as you are, and do not want to invest the time or money building a solution that will not be implemented.

## Known Potential Options for Solving the Need

A key element of the initial business case should include the various potential solutions – at least at a high level. At this point, it is widely understood you are still vetting the potential solutions and providers. But, if you have done your due diligence in identifying potential solutions and partners, you should at least have an idea of what might be available to solve the need. It is ok that these are high-level and include ball-park estimates on cost to your company along with time to implement.

## Do You Have the Time?

It is no secret that organizations are constantly looking to do more with fewer resources and less cost. This means each of us now has more on our plates than we did a year, or five years ago. I shudder when I think of all the resources we had at our fingertips when I first started in sales. But, I wouldn't trade the technology and approach to business that we have today for what it was like so many years ago.

Given that everyone has busy schedules, understanding whether your organization and project team members can invest the time to source and select a solution is a key starting point. This is also a critical element for the provider community. As a member of that club, I can tell when the company does not have commitment from the project team members. It shows up in members not attending meetings, unreasonable internal technology costs, pushed out scheduled dates, and ultimately a cancelled project.

In today's business environment, technology has become one of the leading control points in deciding if a company has the time or interest to commit to a project. Most internal IT departments are stretched very thin, and have a long list of projects awaiting their attention. As a result, IT may associate what seems like an unreasonable number of hours to a specific request. This may be because it is difficult to know the actual number of required hours or, that the internal resources and available time don't exist. So, outsourcing the project, or other projects in order to free up time could be adding to the cost. To be honest, I am not in a position to evaluate whether assigned IT hours are right or wrong. But, I have seen a number of projects come to a screeching halt as the result of IT costs or lack of resources.

In one project I was involved with, a large regional bank wanted to outsource its internal print communications center. During the current state assessment and strategy build, I asked about their budget from an IT perspective to handle the data moving from their internal operation to our platform. This was an area they had thought about, but had not yet had any meaningful conversations with their IT department. I encouraged them to begin those conversations quickly, as I knew from previous experience, this could derail the project. The IT department took more time than any of us anticipated trying to develop the costs. Part of this included a number of meetings my team had with their programmers. Finally, the estimate was returned to the sourcing team. It came in at 11,500 hours, at a cost of $100/hour; $1.15 million of unplanned expense. Even without a financial business case, I knew this project would not get off the ground. I advised the sourcing team that unless there was a more effective approach to addressing the IT development hours, we should jointly agree to shelve the project. And, that is what happened.

Nobody wants to invest themselves, if you cannot garner the time to make a go of the project. Determine this as soon as you can. If it is a go, make certain the project team members understand their participation is imperative, if not required.

## Financially, Is It Worth It?

Some of the most excited conversations I have witnessed, and even participated in, surround the early evaluation of whether solving for a need makes financial sense. This is the point where you have to ensure that qualitative desire matches up with quantitative data. Better that you identify this early in the process than get all the way to the end, only to realize your sourcing team and company do not have the appetite or budget to pay for the solution.

On the other side of the table, potential providers also want to know if you believe pursuing a solution is financially worth it. But, that's not all they are thinking about. Potential providers are evaluating their own ability to help you solve the need, and be selected as your partner. If it's not financially rewarding to the provider, they will abandon the opportunity or try and substitute the optimal solution with something potentially less desirable.

If we are honest with ourselves, we have all looked at a need and continued working to identify a solution long past any reasonable point of continuation. Don't let your passion for a specific need cloud your vision on what may not be financially feasible.

We have a lot of discussions in my company about how to best solution a need for customers. Inevitably, technology bubbles to the surface as a key point – everyone wants to automate the manual processes. As a society, we have become so engrained in technology, that we now approach every need with some level of desired automation. But, financially it may not be worth it. We have actually provided recommendations where a step backward to a manual process is the proposed solution. Sometimes the labor to manage the automated solution, or cost to build the technology, can dwarf any received value. In those cases, a manual or "old school" approach may actually be the best recommendation.

# Cost Benefit Analysis

Following the initial business case, a detailed Cost Benefit Analysis (CBA) or Return on Investment (ROI) is necessary to evaluate the impact to your company. This is generally part of the final recommended solution or options that you may be considering. Different than the initial business case, the CBA is driven almost entirely by the finances of the deal. This is not to suggest that meaningful business requirements are not feeding the model, but the effort is to determine the financial impact of the proposed solution.

In reviewing a proposed solution many companies will make decisions based solely on a positive CBA or ROI. While this should be an important part of the consideration, solving the need may be worth an investment that does not necessarily yield a positive financial outcome. In other words, it may be good for the business, but not necessarily the wallet. At the end of the day, all businesses have to make money in order to survive. So, continually investing in solutions that do not provide a positive ROI is a short-lived strategy. But, sometimes investing in a solution that may not make good financial sense on its own, could positively impact other areas of the organization. Only you will know whether pursing a solution is worth the investment.

At the point you are ready to begin building a financial model of the potential solution, it is imperative to engage the finance resources of your company and the potential partners. By this point, you should have reduced the potential providers to a short list of no more than two or three. In some cases, it may be one provider you choose to work with. Regardless, having the finance folks from both organizations involved early in building the financial model will greatly improve the process. This is the only way to truly understand how each company views various aspects of the cost structure. Both viewpoints are necessary as you work to financially understand the current state and the recommended solution.

Not only is it important to engage the finance resources from both companies, it is equally beneficial to do this early in the process. In fact, it often makes sense to include these two departments as far back as the point of building the initial business case. The quicker you involve both finance organizations, the better alignment you will have when evaluating the solutions.

There are two approaches you can take in building a financial model. Either each side provides limited and protected information or, you both agree to full transparency. When either side chooses to share limited information, it can lead to misinterpretations and incorrect assumptions. For data that we don't know, we fill in with interpreted or assumed input. This can lead to surprises – either immediately or down the road. With full transparency, both parties completely understand the current state and recommended solution costs. This means both companies have to be willing to openly share. Then, in the end there are no surprises on what will happen financially. Even when there are assumptions, both sides are fully aware – and can document this so that when reviewed there is a complete understanding.

Although it may be contrary to your company's culture, strive to work toward full transparency. It can be difficult but, the risk is actually fairly low and the reward of knowing the financial model has been evaluated in full light will pay dividends – well past implementation.

Since I have built a number of financial models surrounding various recommended solutions, I consider myself a master at the process. Because I know my solutions so well, and from various customers I have learned the financial pitfalls to look for, I generally know how to address common concerns that may arise from a financial review.

For this reason, I do not hesitate to ask customers upfront for the complete financials on the current state. This often starts with me asking for a detailed financial statement, or Budget and Expense (B&E) for the current operation. The first time I asked for this information, I thought my boss was going to come unglued. I was in front of the customer, and just asked for the data. I then advised, if it would be helpful, I would provide a spreadsheet template for the desired financial elements. If facial expressions could have communicated what my boss was thinking at that moment, I would have been terminated before we left the building. But, to his surprise, the customer gladly agreed to provide the requested information. Outside of the current vendor spend that had to be masked – because of a non-disclosure agreement, I received the complete data download.

Today, in every opportunity with which I am involved, I ask for detailed financial information covering the current state. If available, it is rare that a customer will not provide it. In fact, I receive more surprised looks from my own staff than I do from customers. When a customer bristles at the request, I work to overcome the objections by explaining the value for both of us. In spite of this, there are occasions when a company just isn't willing or comfortable enough to provide the financial data. In those situations, I probably don't have the optimal solution.

In one opportunity, I was working with a consultant on a BPO initiative for an investment firm. The executive sponsor of the firm was extremely supportive of providing any information we asked for. But, the consultant, who was our day-to-day contact, would ultimately be the one to provide the information. When I asked the consultant for specific budget and expense data of the current state operation, he declined to provide it. He advised that was "proprietary information."

Perhaps he really meant that it was confidential. Or, maybe he didn't have the authority to provide the raw data we had asked for.

As our discussions continued, the consultant told us that if we asked specific questions he would likely be able to answer us – and in most cases this would allow us to land on a fairly good understanding of their current costs. Rather than argue the point, or escalate to the executive sponsor, we used his approach. It seemed a bit backward, and took more time than I had hoped for. But, we built the cost model with certain assumptions and then tweaked it until the consultant advised us we were where we needed to be.

In the end, the consultant understood that to evaluate whether or not there was a business case to support a recommended solution, we had to know the current state costs. Neither of us wanted to spend an inordinate amount of time building a solution that financially was not doable.

The ideal financial model contains three different, sequential components: current state, recommended solution and cost benefit. At its simplest level, the current state compared to the recommended solution yields the cost benefit to the organization. There are levels of detail under each of these categories – specifically the first two. But, in the end the cost benefit is in creating a recommended solution that financially outperforms the current state.

**Figure 6.2 – Cost Benefit Analysis Model**

In establishing the financial model, you can take either a short-term or an extended view. A short-term view is a one-year comparison of the current state to the proposed solution – at full operating speed. This means the potential solution is measured as if it has been implemented when compared to the current state over the same time period. This can often be short-sighted, and eliminates the ramp-up effect that a transition from the current state to the optimal solution can have.

Another consideration is the residual value, or soft dollars, a solution will provide. While the financial model can be fairly black and white, most business decisions are not. It is reasonable to expect that residual value can play an important role in helping determine a go-forward decision. Therefore, you may want to consider some flexibility in the components that comprise the financial model – as long as it makes sense for your company.

The optimal approach is to measure the current state to the recommended solution over a period of three to five years. Three years is on the low side – while five is optimal. This allows you plenty of time to measure the current state in the first year, and any ordinary investments you would have to make if you chose to maintain a status quo. It also provides a vehicle to evaluate the impact of implementation in the first year that can ultimately ramp up to a full run rate in subsequent years.

For nearly half my career I focused only on the one-year comparison model. I always discounted the impact of investment in the current state or any implementation costs in the recommended strategy. This was mostly because there was no place in my model to accommodate it. Twelve months does not provide the runway to show this kind of cost element and demonstrate a favorable return on investment.

As I was presenting my standard one-year model to a hospital in Dallas, TX, I was faced with a senior partner from one of the top ten consulting firms. He had been retained by the hospital to help source their communications and marketing materials that were being produced internally – and at great expense. Following my presentation, he asked if I would meet him for dinner later that evening, just the two of us. Since we were both from out of town, I figured dinner with the consultant would be a better alternative than room service. Adding to my intrigue was that he wanted to meet with me privately, and without his client.

Prior to ordering dinner, the consultant took a bar napkin and began scribbling a conceptual financial model. He then turned the napkin toward me so that I could see a five-year model as opposed to the one-year I had presented earlier in the day. He looked me square in the eye and said, "A one-year CBA does not provide a strong enough business case to support your offer. If you want to continue selling your services with an ROI model, you better start looking at it over a period of three to five years." From the discussion I knew he had confidence in our solution – but that we had applied such a narrow financial model that it weakened the benefit. It was just as important to him as it was to me to ensure the model fairly represented the recommendation. The consultant went on to tell me that all of his clients look at multi-year models to make serious financial decisions.

I then took the model I presented earlier and reworked it into a five-year analysis – this time on my own napkin. Not only was the model more realistic, but it demonstrated the positive financial impact over a longer and more representative period of time. It was simply a better story for me and the hospital. Without any doubt, that was one of those moments in my career when the lightbulb came on – a true paradigm shift. I remember driving back to the hotel after dinner wondering how I had missed something so obvious, for so many years. Today I use that very same model for all of my clients: current state, recommended solution and cost benefit. And, after all these years, I still have the bar napkin!

## Figure 6.3 – Cost Benefit Analysis Model

Current State: Cash Flow With Current Operations (000's)

| In-House Managed Program | Year 1 | Year 2 | Year 3 | Year 4 | Year 5 |
|---|---|---|---|---|---|
| Direct Expense (Production Cost) | $ 18,250 | $ 18,798 | $ 19,361 | $ 19,942 | $ 20,541 |
| Total Compensation | $ 10,000 | $ 10,300 | $ 10,609 | $ 10,927 | $ 11,255 |
| Depreciation | $ 1,500 | $ 1,545 | $ 1,591 | $ 1,639 | $ 1,688 |
| Equipment & Software | $ 3,000 | $ 3,090 | $ 3,183 | $ 3,278 | $ 3,377 |
| Consumables | $ 3,250 | $ 3,348 | $ 3,448 | $ 3,551 | $ 3,658 |
| Other | $ 500 | $ 515 | $ 530 | $ 546 | $ 563 |
| Indirect Expense | $ 9,500 | $ 9,785 | $ 10,079 | $ 10,381 | $ 10,692 |
| Client Service Delivery | $ 5,000 | $ 5,150 | $ 5,305 | $ 5,464 | $ 5,628 |
| Engineering | $ 1,000 | $ 1,030 | $ 1,061 | $ 1,093 | $ 1,126 |
| Product Relationship Management | $ 1,200 | $ 1,236 | $ 1,273 | $ 1,311 | $ 1,351 |
| Supply Chain Management | $ 1,300 | $ 1,339 | $ 1,379 | $ 1,421 | $ 1,463 |
| Executive Admin | $ 1,000 | $ 1,030 | $ 1,061 | $ 1,093 | $ 1,126 |
| TOTAL | $ 27,750 | $ 28,583 | $ 29,440 | $ 30,323 | $ 31,233 |
| Cumulative Totals | $ 27,750 | $ 56,333 | $ 85,772 | $ 116,096 | $ 147,329 |

Recommended Solution: Potential Cash Flow With Transformation Strategy (000's)

| In-House Managed Program | Year 1 | Year 2 | Year 3 | Year 4 | Year 5 |
|---|---|---|---|---|---|
| Direct Expense (Production Cost) | $ 10,038 | $ 7,550 | $ - | $ - | $ - |
| Total Compensation | $ 5,500 | $ 4,000 | $ - | $ - | $ - |
| Depreciation | $ 825 | $ 600 | $ - | $ - | $ - |
| Equipment & Software | $ 1,650 | $ 1,250 | $ - | $ - | $ - |
| Consumables | $ 1,788 | $ 1,500 | $ - | $ - | $ - |
| Other | $ 275 | $ 200 | $ - | $ - | $ - |
| Indirect Expense | $ 5,225 | $ 2,275 | $ - | $ - | $ - |
| Client Service Delivery | $ 2,750 | $ 450 | $ - | $ - | $ - |
| Engineering | $ 550 | $ 540 | $ - | $ - | $ - |
| Product Relationship Management | $ 660 | $ 585 | $ - | $ - | $ - |
| Supply Chain Management | $ 715 | $ 450 | $ - | $ - | $ - |
| Executive Admin | $ 550 | $ 250 | $ - | $ - | $ - |
| Implementation / Transition | $ 1,000 | $ 750 | $ - | $ - | $ - |
| Sub Total | $ 16,263 | $ 10,575 | $ - | $ - | $ - |

| Outsourced Managed Program | Year 1 | Year 2 | Year 3 | Year 4 | Year 5 |
|---|---|---|---|---|---|
| **Program Expenses** | $ 3,504 | $ 3,197 | $ 745 | $ 768 | $ 791 |
| Implementation / Transition | $ 1,200 | $ 1,000 | $ - | $ - | $ - |
| Platform Setup / Implementation | $ 1,100 | $ 1,000 | $ - | $ - | $ - |
| Training | $ 125 | $ 100 | $ - | $ - | $ - |
| Platform License and Maintenance | $ 50 | $ 52 | $ 53 | $ 55 | $ 56 |
| Application Development | $ 900 | $ 927 | $ 650 | $ 670 | $ 690 |
| Sales Tax | $ 129 | $ 119 | $ 42 | $ 43 | $ 45 |
| **Operating Expenses** | | | | | |
| **Direct Expense (Production Cost)** | $ 8,178 | $ 9,100 | $ 19,475 | $ 18,996 | $ 18,426 |
| File Ingestion / Record Processing | $ 1,000 | $ 1,200 | $ 2,250 | $ 2,183 | $ 2,117 |
| Print Production | $ 2,750 | $ 2,500 | $ 5,000 | $ 4,850 | $ 4,705 |
| Presort / Comingle | $ 650 | $ 750 | $ 1,500 | $ 1,455 | $ 1,411 |
| Electronic File Conversion | $ 225 | $ 275 | $ 525 | $ 509 | $ 494 |
| Certified Mail | $ 90 | $ 110 | $ 200 | $ 194 | $ 188 |
| Paper and Envelopes | $ 2,000 | $ 2,250 | $ 5,750 | $ 5,578 | $ 5,410 |
| Kitting & Fulfillment | $ 750 | $ 1,000 | $ 2,500 | $ 2,425 | $ 2,352 |
| Storage | $ 250 | $ 500 | $ 750 | $ 728 | $ 706 |
| Sales Tax | $ 463 | $ 515 | $ 1,000 | $ 1,075 | $ 1,043 |
| **Program Management** | $ 2,000 | $ 2,000 | $ 2,060 | $ 1,998 | $ 1,938 |
| **Client Services** | $ 1,000 | $ 1,000 | $ 2,500 | $ 2,425 | $ 2,352 |
| **Executive Admin** | $ 100 | $ 150 | $ 200 | $ 200 | $ 200 |
| **Sub Total** | $ 14,782 | $ 15,447 | $ 24,980 | $ 24,387 | $ 23,707 |
| | | | | | |
| **TOTAL** | $ 31,044 | $ 26,022 | $ 24,980 | $ 24,387 | $ 23,707 |
| **Cumulative Totals** | $ 31,044 | $ 46,492 | $ 71,472 | $ 95,859 | $ 119,566 |

Cost Benefit of Recommended Solution (000's)

| Comparison | Year 1 | Year 2 | Year 3 | Year 4 | Year 5 |
|---|---|---|---|---|---|
| Current State | $ 27,750 | $ 28,583 | $ 29,440 | $ 30,323 | $ 31,233 |
| Recommended Solution | $ 31,044 | $ 26,022 | $ 24,980 | $ 24,387 | $ 23,707 |
| | | | | | |
| **Annual % Improvement** | -11.87% | 8.96% | 15.15% | 19.58% | 24.10% |
| **Annual $$ Improvement** | $ (3,294) | $ 2,560 | $ 4,460 | $ 5,936 | $ 7,526 |
| **Cumulative $$ Improvement** | $ (3,294) | $ (734) | $ 3,726 | $ 9,662 | $ 17,188 |

**Assumptions - Current State**

- Both models include only the current in-house program components.
- Includes a 3% increase in costs year-over-year.
- Does not include rent, utilities, and other building-related overhead.
- Does not take into consideration capital investment or lease-renewals that will be required if in-house program remains.

**Assumptions - Recommended Solution**

- In favor of electronic communications, demand for printed materials will likely decrease over the course of five years, but is not factored into the model.
- Does not include Postage, but may be positively impacted as the result of the Recommended Strategy.

The above sample model does not represent any specific customer. Rather, it demonstrates some of the best components from several models over a number of years. While the CBA may seem somewhat intimidating at first, if you step back and look at it from a high-level, you will see the simplicity begin to emerge. It contains the three elements described above and, each category is reviewed across a period of five years.

To better understand the model, and how it is built, let's review each section in more detail.

## Current State

The current state takes a look at the operation as it exists today, over a five-year period. Some of the information shown in the model is similar to a B&E statement for a customer considering a recommended solution to outsource their internal marketing communications services. As a result, many of the categories are as the customer might define them in the B&E. When presented back, it is familiar territory for them to understand. This is important not only for understanding the current state, but for later comparing it to the recommended solution.

In the demonstration model, there are two categories of current state spend: direct and indirect. Direct are all of the expenses associated with manufacturing the marketing communications that are created and mailed from the company's in-house operation. This is mostly direct labor, equipment and consumable materials. Direct expenses are fairly easy to wrap your head around.

Indirect expenses, on the other hand, can be a bit more complicated. These include cost elements required to run the business, but don't necessarily contribute directly to the creation of the marketing communications. The example includes client services, engineering (the development of new processes and workflow models), product relationship, supply chain management, and executive management overhead.

You may have noticed that rent, utilities and building-related overhead are missing from the model. For as many models as I have prepared, at least half of the customers' finance organizations removed these categories. I have learned that this particular area of expense can be an emotional topic. Many believe that rent, utilities and overhead are fixed costs. And, that unless you can eliminate the expense completely (or the portion applied to the current state), then you cannot effectively consider it in the analysis. On the other hand, just as many think the costs are real and represent contributing factors to the current state financial model. I can actually see both sides of this position. But, generally I believe that in comparison to the recommended solution, which often will include rent, utilities and building-related overhead, inclusion in the current state makes sense. In your situation, you will have to decide.

At the bottom of the current state, you will see totals for each year. And, below that is the cumulative spend. This is where I typically migrate when reviewing the financial viability of a recommended solution in comparison to the current state.

It is important to note that soft dollars are not included anywhere in the CBA. Soft dollars are those elements of a current state or recommended solution that add residual value – such as workflow improvement, increased efficiency, or ease of doing business. But, they stop short of offering any financial impact to the model. As tempting as it may be to include soft costs, work to refrain from doing so. I am relentless about ensuring financial models I work with never include soft dollars. This does not mean you shouldn't include soft dollars in the overall review of the potential solution – they just shouldn't be part of the financial analysis. If you find yourself struggling in this area, rest assured your finance department, or that of the potential partner, will probably eliminate them for you.

At the bottom of the chart I have included assumptions and information related to the financial model. Specifically, there are comments on the current state and the recommended solution. The assumptions should be used to identify areas where components of the model would not otherwise be easily detected, or understood. In the current state, the above model includes a 3% operating cost increase year over year. And, it does not take into account any future investment if the in-house operation continues. For example, equipment replacements, which would be demonstrated as depreciation in the model, are not included. When known, this is a key element that should be included. Required capital investments can greatly impact the outcome of a CBA, and are very real expenses to the continuation of a current state operation. Surprisingly, this is frequently overlooked by companies looking to outsource a currently in-sourced service.

## Recommended Solution

Depending on your company and the specific need / solution you are solving for, your CBA may contain very different categories. Let's go through the components shown in the recommended solution section of the model.

The recommended solution contains two categories of data. The first is the continuation of the in-house operation. The second is the outsourced program, which came from the recommended solution presented to the customer.

In many scenarios, there will be a run-down of the current state and a ramp-up of the go-forward program. Here, the implementation is anticipated to take just shy of 24 months to fully complete. Thus, you see costs to run the in-house operation until the outsource solution is completely operational. The categories of direct and indirect expense match those of the current state. And, in most instances the financial costs are similar. But, there is a scaled reduction of expenses in years 1 and 2 as the transition to the outsourced solution occurs. Then, in years 3, 4 and 5 these expenses are eliminated.

By contrast, the outsourced managed program shows a ramp-up in expenses for the first two years before the program becomes fully operational in year 3.

In the recommended solution section, you will see implementation costs for both the in-house and outsourced operations. This is because there are anticipated costs to shut down the internal operation, and then additional implementation expenses with the transition to the outsourced solution.

The outsourced managed program identifies two categories of expenses: program and operating. The program expenses are the implementation costs, technology establishment, platform licensing and management, and application development. Note that platform licensing and application development have on-going costs throughout the life of the program.

Operating expenses are the costs to run the solution on a daily basis. These include the direct expense to manufacture, program management, client services and executive administration to oversee the program. Although not easily identified in the model, executive administration includes internal resources to the company, whereas the other expenses are directly related to the outsourced solution, and billable from the solution provider.

Similar to the current state section, the recommended solution contains totals, both annually and then cumulative across the five-year period. As with the current state, I begin to quickly focus my attention on the five-year cumulative total.

The recommended solution also contains assumptions which are footnoted at the bottom of the chart. An important note here is the focused elimination of printed communication materials in favor of alternative channels that the current state does not offer.

## Cost Benefit

Following the current state and recommended solution sections, the critical piece of the CBA is the actual cost benefit. This is the section that analyses the financial benefit of the solution as compared to the current state.

The first part of the cost benefit is a simple financial comparison between the current state and the recommended solution. It is the same formula presented earlier: current state − recommended solution = cost benefit.

The three rows below that provide insight into the model across the five-year span. The first is an annual percentage improvement which looks at each year independently to determine the financial impact, or cost benefit, in each program year. Underneath that are the dollars associated with the difference between the current state and the recommended solution. The final row demonstrates the cumulative financial improvement of the solution. As before, I quickly navigate to the five-year cumulative dollar improvement.

Depending on the need, the current state environment and the complexity of the recommended solution, I have differing views on what makes for a good business case to make a move. The more complex and time consuming a solution migration will be, the better the ROI needs to be. If the effort and cost to move to the recommended solution is low, then the ROI doesn't have to be as strong. Do not to focus solely on the percentage line or the dollars. Sometimes the percentage of the cost benefit may appear low, but the dollars returned to the organization are substantial. All of these are key discussion points to have both internally and with your potential provider. Remember, if selected your partner will have as much skin in the game as you do.

---

Be careful not to let the financial analysis paralyze you, the project team or the potential providers. You may have heard this referred to as "analysis paralysis." Analysis paralysis can quickly derail your initiative by shifting the focus to only the numbers − and not the desired solution.

Granted, all solutions should have a financial analysis performed – but other considerations may be important as well. This includes the primary objective of understanding if you can solve for what may be a significant need in your company.

One of the more challenging financial business cases I worked on was with a Midwest retail bank. They were looking at outsourcing their internal print and mail operation – and as part of the solution a workflow process that allowed their customers to choose their preferred means of communication. This meant a shift toward streams other than printed bank statements and notices. The challenging part was it would be almost entirely self-directed by the bank's customers. This was something they had never done before – in fact the bank had no idea if it could be accomplished with complete autonomy and direction by their customers.

During the RFI no business case was performed. And, the subsequent RFP only briefly addressed it at a very high level. As I think about it now, the process during the RFP was more aligned with what I would ordinarily expect in an RFI. The deep dive on the financial cost benefit was performed as the bank was narrowing down to a final decision.

To begin the process, I used the template shared above. The bank quickly adopted my format, but was selective about what they chose to share with me on their operating costs. I captured what I understood about the financial aspects of the bank's current state, including investment costs I knew they would have if they decided to keep their operation inside. I then developed the go-forward model if we were to perform the proposed outsourced program. Included in this was the cost of transition, professional fees and operational costs to manage the program. While I intimately knew my costs associated with the recommended solution, I had little insight into their current costs. As I would present versions of spreadsheets to the bank, they would ask for a conference call and then dig into details surrounding specific components of the pricing model. It wasn't uncommon for them to ask for a meeting with no preparation materials provided, and then pop up a spreadsheet via WebEx™ with a variety of questions. When I would ask for numbers or detail on their side, it was generally met with some level of resistance. Because I had little insight into their actual financial model, I could only speculate as to what issues they kept uncovering.

Finally, it reached a point where the bank knew they had to begin sharing some of the information that had previously been highly protected. Several months passed before they provided abbreviated information. And, the data they were sharing was aggregated numbers with little detail. They removed formulas and links to what appeared to be outside spreadsheets – one in particular being the master model. With each round of spreadsheet, both the bank and I had more questions. In spite of repeatedly asking that we all work from the same spreadsheet, with full disclosure, it never happened. Rather, the bank spent an inordinate amount of time coming back to us with different scenarios – asking for the impact to our pricing structure. While I had an idea of the gap they were trying to solve, I wasn't sure I completely understood the financial objectives of the initiative. As a result, it proved challenging to help them get to the desired end state. When I asked about the overall financial goal and gaps they were struggling with, I was only told that the solution had to pay for itself in the first year. As you can imagine, this was a huge challenge.

While the financial modeling and tweaking of the recommended solution were occurring, the in-house operation was having performance issues with its equipment. We learned that most of it was well past its useful life, and some was in jeopardy of no longer being serviced by the equipment provider. Further, it was breaking down on a daily basis causing missed commitments of delivering communications to its customers. This was adding pressure to the sourcing team to make a "go" or "no-go" decision of our recommended solution.

Still, the financial modeling continued ad nauseam. I lost count of the number of models, conference calls and in-person meetings where we reviewed various scenarios and worked through spreadsheets.

As a result of the equipment failure, and the associated risk, the head of that department approached the bank's executives with his serious, and legitimate, concerns. He advised that the project team had been unable to reach a decision – and it had worked for months without a solid direction. His recommendation was to replace the equipment and continue operating the internal print and mail center – without outsourcing. Essentially, he suggested the project team scrap its efforts.

After nearly 24 months of work, the executives agreed, and the project was abandoned. The bank decided there was no plausible way, in the current environment, to outsource with the financial outcomes the organization desired. While there may have been a way to get there, the time spent and struggle to share information in an open environment resulted in a "no-go." Once again, status quo won the deal. This time the customer *and* I lost. But, the bank's customers also lost. The opportunity for them to be able to receive communications in any manner they chose, as opposed to how the bank can deliver in the current state (mostly in print), was eliminated. Although I have no way to quantify it, I suspect there was also an impact to the bank for the lost opportunity of better connecting with their customers.

The financial business case, at both levels: the initial business case and the cost benefit analysis, is a must-have in evaluating potential solutions and partners to address your need. Whether you use the model provided here, prefer one you have built in your own organization, or utilize a version from your potential partner, spend the time to thoroughly complete the CBA. Include your internal team as well as the potential providers in the process. Do this with an open book – on both sides of the table. The more open you are, the more beneficial the CBA will be. And, engage the finance organizations, internally and externally, early in the process.

---

# Key Points

- A critical element for both the company and the provider community is to understand whether there is a financial business case for solving a need.

- There are two levels of a financial business case:
  - Initial business case – a high-level determination of whether you should invest in pursuing a solution and engaging potential partners.
  - Cost benefit analysis – a financial deep dive into determining whether the optimal solution and potential partner will provide the desired financial payback or cost benefit if implemented. This is typically performed at the point of identifying one or two potential providers.
- Parts of the initial business case:
  - Define the need
  - What if you don't solve the need?
  - Know potential options for solving the need
  - Do you have the time?
  - Financially is it worth it?
- Following the initial business case, a detailed Cost Benefit Analysis (CBA) or Return on Investment (ROI) is necessary to evaluate the impact to your company. A CBA can best be defined as an assessment of the current state compared to a recommended solution which yields the cost benefit.
- Do not to let the financial analysis paralyze you, the project team or the potential providers. This can quickly derail your initiative by shifting the focus to only the numbers – and not the desired solution.

# 7
# SELECTING THE RIGHT PARTNER

Once you have vetted the potential solutions and providers in the market place, along with the financial analyses or CBA, it's time to make a decision. On the surface this seems like it would be an easy task. Sometimes it is. The obvious choice may bubble right up to the surface. But, more times than not there will be two or more providers that can solve the need. More specifically, there may be elements of each one that you like – and you only wish you could merge the good qualities or components together and build the perfect provider. Unfortunately, if you are looking for a sole provider to solve the need, you are going to have to choose.

## Formal Written Proposal

Regardless of the process you use, whether an RFP or other means of soliciting a proposal, a formal written proposal from the potential provider, or providers, is a good idea. When referring to a formal written proposal, this includes a free format (i.e. Word document), a filled in template such as Excel, or a completed e-procurement tool. In any selected format, the formal proposal should contain details of the solution / recommended approach along with the financial costs and benefits, and the process to implement the solution.

A key component I try to include in formal proposals is a gap analysis. This is generally a table that identifies specific elements of the current state, the recommended go-forward solution for each element, the risk (or gap), and the required mitigation. In all cases I include gaps on both sides of the table. The goal is to identify things that could be potential barriers or show-stoppers to the solution's success. Following is a simple example of a Gap Analysis.

### Figure 7.1 – Gap Analysis

| Current State | Required State | Risk | Mitigation |
|---|---|---|---|
| Internal IT resources have multiple strategic initiatives in progress. | Collaboration on development and migration priorities. Co-architecture integration between two companies. Development, integration and migration to a new strategic partner, and other BU specific initiatives. | Stalled implementation and migration of the work to the new solution. | ABC Company must commit time and resources early to document and compile collaborative plan. Potential provider to offer staff augmentation resources to assist. |
| Currently, there are several lines of business receiving a high level of service from ABC Company employees that have tremendous "tribal knowledge." | Migration of knowledge and people, where necessary, to maintain level of service, knowledge and understanding of ABC Company's business. | Reduced knowledge and service levels impacting the success of the program and ABC Company adoption of potential provider. | Immediate strategy around job shadowing and potential rebadging key ABC Company personnel. Executive sponsorship required to broker close relationships with key employees and business units. |

| Current State | Required State | Risk | Mitigation |
|---|---|---|---|
| Currently, ABC Company's internal solution is a very established stable environment that has been built around the very specific needs of ABC Company. | Potential provider achieves their goal of seamless transition of the work into their environment. | Timelines, architecture, personnel, and/or application complexity can cause business disruption. | Potential provider and ABC Company to establish highly cross-functional teams with executive sponsorship to manage issues, initiate a documented corrective action plan, and expedite project resolution; clear lines of communication established between all stakeholders. |

Ultimately the formal written proposal has to be one of the key elements in selecting the final solution and partner.

# Formal Presentation of the Solution

In many sourcing initiatives the formal written proposal is followed by a presentation of the recommended solution. I have been involved in initiatives where a formal presentation is not included. This is sometimes the case when the solution is fairly simple. If the solution is more complex, a decision to exclude presentations may not be a good approach.

Formal presentations allow the potential providers to verbally present the recommended solution, their company and team. It also gives you a chance to better understand the proposal – and ask questions. As much as you may think you understand the written proposal – there are likely assumptions on both sides that may result in a slanted view of the recommended solution. Often this can be easily clarified through verbal interaction. For these reasons, I strongly encourage formal presentations be included as part of the process.

As a sales executive there are two key points that always come to mind regarding the formal presentation:

1. Will my company be invited to present?
2. How much time will be allotted for the presentation?

If after a potential provider submits a proposal, the company is not invited to make a formal presentation – the assumption by the sales executive is the deal is over. And, in most cases this is probably spot on. It's reasonable to assume that not every provider who submits a proposal will be invited to present. I certainly understand the sourcing team may not have the kind of time necessary to sit through presentations from every respondent to an RFP. When this is the case, communicate to the impacted providers and explain they have not been selected to move forward. Even if you think there is an outside chance you may want to later reignite conversations – tell them where they stand!

You are probably thinking, "Great, now I have to listen to the sales executive tell me why they should be included in the formal presentation …and what a terrible mistake my team has made." And, you know what? You are right! Any sales executive worth their salt will plead their case to present. Use this opportunity to explain why the potential provider was not invited. This is not a time to give a vague answer. A response like, "Your company just does not fit the standard we are looking for" is not helpful. Be very specific as to why the provider was not selected to move forward. Then, listen to the sales executive. They may have a very good response. In fact, you may find that after the conversation it is worth reconsidering. If you are on the fence about a potential provider – include them in the presentations. Don't be influenced by a process that, for example, says you only have room for three companies to present. It would be a disappointing outcome if a potential provider was eliminated because of a misinterpretation of their proposal that could have been cleared up during the oral presentation.

As a sales executive, I rarely think there is enough time allotted for the formal presentations. But, on the other hand, I have heard many sourcing executives express that often too much time is spent on this piece of the puzzle. I'm not sure if there is any middle ground on this one. But, I do believe there has to be sufficient time for the potential provider to adequately present the story – while still allowing much needed feedback and discussion from the sourcing team.

Typically, I see a formal presentation meeting invitation for a very specific amount of time. This is generally accompanied by an agenda indicating what the sourcing team would like to see. The agenda might include topics such as background on the company, review of the current state analysis, presentation of the recommended solution, and what it takes to get from the proposal stage to an implemented solution. For the most part, this makes sense.

Where this gets off track is when not enough time is allocated, or the agenda is compartmentalized and rigid to the point it erodes any value of having an in-person presentation. For this reason, I find it best if you allot enough time (let's say two hours as a starting point), provide a high-level agenda guideline, allow the providers a certain level of autonomy to present what they believe matters, and then encourage questions *during* the meeting (not at the end). Certainly you want to convey the important topics to be addressed. But, there is no need to spoon feed the process. And, don't worry about not finishing in time. If you can't get it done, schedule some more time!

A few years ago my team and I were working on a Business Process Outsourcing (BPO) initiative for a public university in the Midwest. We had completed the current state assessment, provided the written proposal and were scheduled to deliver the formal presentation to the sourcing team and business stakeholders. For the most part, the stakeholders included the various colleges and functional departments. Prior to the presentation, they provided a detailed agenda – which included a play-by-play for one and a half hours. Here is what it looked like:

| | | |
|---|---|---|
| 1:00 pm – 1:05 pm | - | Introductions |
| 1:05 pm – 1:10 pm | - | Company background |
| 1:10 pm – 1:25 pm | - | Current state assessment |
| 1:25 pm – 1:45 pm | - | Recommended solution |
| 1:45 pm – 2:05 pm | - | Technology demo |
| 2:05 pm – 2:15 pm | - | Implementation / Account management team |
| 2:15 pm – 2:20 pm | - | Contract review |
| 2:20 pm – 2:30 pm | - | Questions from sourcing team and stakeholders |

A rather packed agenda. I called the sourcing executive and expressed concern around being able to get through the agenda in one and a half hours. He advised this was all any provider was being allowed and recommended we do the best we could.

We got into the presentation, and launched a few minutes late because not all of the sourcing team was on time. As we began tackling the agenda topics, multiple interruptions came from the sourcing team and stakeholders. Rightfully so, they were asking a lot of really good questions. Interaction during a presentation is much preferred to the stoic group who saves their questions until the end. From my perspective the sourcing team and stakeholders were interested in our recommended solution and very engaged in an active discussion.

Shortly after 2:00 pm, the sourcing executive called for a "time check" and advised that there were less than twenty minutes remaining before the Q&A portion of the meeting; even though we started late and questions had been peppered throughout. But, since I diligently watch the clock during presentations, I knew where we were in terms of time. And, I also knew we would not get all the way through the agenda. As best we could, we continued on. I picked up the pace, and just before 2:20, I moved the presentation into a wrap-up so that I could turn it over to the sourcing team right on schedule.

As is standard practice for me, the next day I called the sourcing executive to ask how the presentation was received. He advised that we were the third group to present in a line-up of five potential partners who had been invited in. And, up to this point all three had come up short on completely hitting the agenda topics. He expressed disappointment – and perhaps some concern that their team was not gaining the benefit he had hoped.

The sourcing executive realized the issue was too much requested material in too little time. I suggested he pick the providers whose solutions and teams seemed the best fit and invite them in for a second meeting. I also suggested that the meetings be more of a round table discussion, to cover any key points that had been missed during the presentations, and to dig deeper into each of the recommended solutions. I then encouraged him to allot an appropriate amount of time such that he and his team received the value necessary to ultimately make a decision. And, that is exactly what happened.

This scenario could have been avoided if the agenda was a bit more streamlined (i.e. move the technology demo to another session), and more time had been allotted. A missed opportunity was not asking the potential providers for their input on how the meeting should be structured – and how much time each thought they needed to make their pitch. Imagine how the presentations could have been different (and perhaps better) if the sourcing executive had taken the opportunity to level with the potential providers prior to the meeting – and ask for their input.

# Scoring of the Solutions / Providers

Regardless of the scoring sheet you use, it is important to actually score the potential providers – as objectively as you can. This does not mean the score is the end-all, and should be solely used to determine the final selection. But, it does provide a quantifiable view of the sourcing effort.

To this end, each sourcing team member should evaluate and score the potential solutions and partners independently. It's ok to discuss as a group later; but, the first pass should be completely independent.

Once the scores of the team have been received, the team lead should tally them and prepare a consolidated view of the scores. This can then be used by the sourcing team as one input element to have a discussion on the available options, and ultimately a vote for the final decision.

# Discussion / Voting by the Sourcing Team

I would love to be a fly on the wall for some of the discussions and voting on potential providers and their solutions. But, I have received enough feedback from various companies to know this can be a challenging part of the process.

It makes sense to start with the scoring sheet used in the earlier step. If done correctly, there should be a score for various key elements of the decision-making process. A consolidated tally of the scores should provide a visual comparison of all of the potential providers.

But, this does not always mean the scores alone indicate the best choice. There may be situations where the top scoring solution and partner do not reflect the way you, or others on the sourcing team, really feel. Nor does it mean the score alone should dictate the direction you choose. Regardless of whether it is a clear choice, have a discussion among the sourcing team on how you want to move forward. While the scores should be considered, an oral review provides an opportunity to discuss the options, hear concerns, and learn critical thinking points from the sourcing team as it relates to the recommended solutions. In this discussion, allow each team member to openly share their favorite solution / provider. But, make sure the conversations are defendable. For example, it is insufficient to have a team member say, "I just have a good feeling about this particular provider." Rather, each individual should come prepared to explain why they believe one partner should emerge as the provider of choice.

# Go Back to the Potential Providers for Clarification

After the scoring and discussion session, you may find that you are struggling to make a decision. In fact, the discussion can actually bring out additional questions or thoughts not previously encountered. You may even find that points of clarification are worth answering before selecting the solution and go-forward provider.

When this occurs, go back to the short list of potential providers you are considering – and share with them the concerns, points of clarification or questions you have. You may actually be struggling with issues they can easily help you address – and that they have potentially encountered before. This is one of the times it can pay to be open with the providers and solicit their input to help you make the final decision.

# Make the Selection

There are a number of ways to select the optimal solution and partner. One of the best approaches I heard came from an RFP process neither my company nor I was involved in. A friend of mine, who is a sales executive in IT services, shared the story of a professional services firm that had issued an RFP for a new Enterprise Resource Planning (ERP) platform. It was a large and expensive undertaking for the firm and a significant opportunity for the provider community. A sourcing team of approximately 15 associates from the firm would ultimately make the decision. A scoring sheet was used throughout the process. In addition to the sourcing team, there were two executive sponsors who were expected to be non-voting members of the team.

Prior to meeting for the selection, rules were established that the decision would be by unanimous consensus. Meaning, the team of 15 would have to agree on the optimal solution and provider. In the event there was not a consensus, the team would convene again, discuss what would likely be fewer options, and re-vote. This would continue until all agreed on the solution. In the unlikely event the team could not reach a consensus, the two executive sponsors would step in to help facilitate a unified outcome. And, in a stalemate the executives would make the final decision.

Following the scoring, the team met (without the executive sponsors) and discussed every potential provider. Each team member weighed in on how they felt – and which solution / potential provider they believed offered the best solution. Each provided a detailed explanation supporting their recommendation. It took a couple of rounds, but the group came to a consensus – without the intervention of the executive sponsors.

An interesting side note on this approach: A key element was that once a unified decision had been made, each team member had to fully support that decision. In other words, there could not be any grumbling or bellyaching after the fact unless there was sufficient cause. And, if that did occur – the entire team (including the two executive sponsors) had to reconvene to address how to move forward.

I would only add one thing to this approach. Share, up front, this process with the potential providers! I cannot recall a scenario where I knew that level of detail in the selection process. Not that it would change the outcome – but in the spirit of a true potential partnership it would be nice to know there is a logical approach to selecting the right solution and partner.

# Communicate / Keep Your Options Open

Once a decision is made, it is important to communicate, to all of the providers, the direction you chose. And, I believe it is important to do this as soon as you know.

Too often I encounter situations where the sourcing team "goes dark" during the process of evaluating and selecting a solution and go-forward provider. This means they stop communicating during, and even after, the evaluation and selection process. Specifically, this may include communicating only to the winning partner, and not communicating anything to the others. The result is it leaves the provider community in limbo wondering what is going on.

Once a decision has been reached – even if you have yet to fully negotiate a formal contract, let everyone know. It's ok to let the potential providers know you have reached a *tentative* decision – which will be formalized by a contract. In fact, why not tell each potential provider where they ranked among the competition? I think it is also valuable to advise that in the event a formal agreement cannot be reached, you may be back in touch with them.

Above all else, keep the lines of communication open. Things happen. The selected solution and go-forward provider may not be all that you hoped they would be. You never know when you may need to go back to the potential providers for further discussions – including a potential business relationship.

---

# Key Points

- A formal written proposal from each potential provider is essential to selecting the optimal go-forward partner. Regardless of the format, the document should contain details of the solution / recommended approach, financial costs and benefits, and the process to implement the solution.

- A Gap Analysis, which is generally in the format of a table, should be documented and included in each formal proposal. It identifies elements of the go-forward solution that may require some additional work (the gaps) before implementation. Gaps and recommended remediation pertaining to both parties should be identified.

- Allow the potential providers opportunities to verbally present their proposals. Presentations that encourage interactive oral dialog can ensure clarity on both sides of the table. And, ensure that sufficient time is allotted to those presenting.

- Ask the sourcing team members to review each proposal, score them, discuss among the team, and then vote. There may be times when it is necessary to go back to one or more providers for clarification. When necessary, don't skip this critical step.

- In making a decision, it is best to have a consensus among the sourcing team. And, once a decision is made to move forward – everyone on the sourcing team must support the decision. Before the selection begins, share with the potential providers your criteria and process.

- As soon as reasonably possible, communicate your decision to the provider community. But, keep your options open. You never know when you will need to go back to the provider community and re-engage with one or more potential partner not originally selected to solve the need.
- Communicate frequently with the invited potential providers on where you are in the process.

# 8
# THE CONTRACT

*Disclaimer:* *Although it may appear obvious, I want to be clear that I am not an attorney, and am in no way providing legal advice in any manner, whatsoever. The following is intended to be information based on experiences I have had, and what I believe matters most in contracts I have negotiated – particularly business issues. Please consult your own legal counsel for specifics related to any Agreement you intend to enter into.*

Oftentimes there is anxiety for both sides when it comes time to negotiating a contract. I have a different view. This is the best part of the deal – it means I won! As a customer, this means you have found the right partner and optimal solution! And, since I have never lost an opportunity at this stage of the game, I actually enjoy the process of contract negotiation. Perhaps it is a mindset.

In many situations, the selection of a new partner and solution may mean an impact to existing contracts or current relationships. As I have watched the sourcing process over a period of time, I find it interesting that many companies choose to surprise the incumbent with a new go-forward plan at the last possible minute. This creates anxiety with the current providers, and may even present a difficult situation during a transition to the new solution. Unless there are underlying circumstances where you have relationship or volatile performance issues, it is best to let the incumbents know early in the process that you are exploring a solution that may impact the relationship. In fact, there may even be a potential solution from the incumbent that can address the need. Surprising your current partners adds little value to the process and may do more harm than good.

One of the largest trust banks in the US solicited an RFP for their critical check documents issued to high-wealth customers. The program also managed check distribution for business customers under the customers' names. These checks were for general business transactions – such as bill-pay.

In addition to my company and a few others, the current vendor was part of the RFP process. But, as the process unfolded there was little communication with the incumbent that they might not be selected as the go-forward partner. In the final decision, my company was selected. After successfully negotiating the contract and well into the implementation, my customer decided to finally approach the incumbent vendor to tell them they would not be the go-forward partner. In addition, he provided a timeline of what to expect in terms of transition. It was a staged transition where the business would be moved in two or three waves. The first wave was the largest, and was scheduled inside of 60 days. The second and third waves were scheduled for a final completion of 180 days. After the vendor heard the news, they advised my client that if they moved any part of the business prior to 90 days, they would immediately halt all production, which was a breach of contract.

This left the bank in a bit of a pickle. If they called the vendor's bluff, there might actually be a stop in production impacting thousands of customers – including high-wealth individuals and commercial customers. This was in spite of potential legal action as a result of the incumbent's decision. On the other hand, any delay in executing our newly inked contract would significantly impact the solution. Two main concerns on delaying our program were a significant loss in savings and additional implementation fees. But, at the end of the day, no bank that size is going to run the risk of impacting their customers, not to mention the public relations nightmare it could cause in the media.

You may be thinking this is a very risky move by the current vendor. That thought certainly crossed my mind. I couldn't help but think – and shared this with the bank, that this is a proverbial bridge I would not want to burn if I were in the incumbent's position. And, I have been in that position – where a longstanding customer decides to move in a different direction. My approach has always been to handle such transitions with grace and a maybe a bit of humility. Besides, who knows what the future holds? The contract with the new provider may not play out as expected. Or, in the future I may have a solution that is of interest to the departing customer. I have learned that in business, companies do not easily forget being mistreated to such a degree as described here.

In the end, the executives of the incumbent came to their senses and agreed to honor their existing contract without breach. But, the entire situation startled the bank. As a result, they delayed the transition to the new solution. I wonder if the fire drill and delayed implementation could have been avoided if the bank had been more candid with the incumbent that exiting their current contract was a very real possibility.

The learning experience here, is to be sure you fully understand your current contract before deciding to move away from it. This should occur early in the process – perhaps at the point of identifying your potential providers. Knowing how to exit a current contract – even if it is near expiration, and the risks it imposes will help you plan for and potentially avoid delays in implementing your optimal solution.

# Non-Disclosure Agreements

Over the past few years, Non-Disclosure Agreements (NDAs) have become quite popular – for both companies requiring and selling solutions. Rightfully so, they are intended to protect sensitive data that may be shared during the business relationship. This may be customer specific data that can pose a legal risk to a company or intellectual capital that could otherwise be shared with competitors. In advance of a contract, these documents serve to provide protection for both parties and allow for information sharing.

Many companies have non-disclosure agreement templates already built. And, they are just waiting for certain information to be filled in and then executed.

Outside of ensuring that confidential information is protected, the most important element of the document is to ensure it is bilateral. This means it protects both parties. A unilateral NDA only protects one of the two parties. This is almost always presented by the company seeking the solution. But, it provides a lopsided approach that simply isn't fair. As my dad would often say, "what's good for the goose is good for the gander." Frankly, both parties deserve to have their sensitive data and intellectual property protected.

Whenever I see a unilateral NDA – and one that is presented under the pretext that it cannot be modified, the decision to move forward becomes questionable for me. Since NDAs are often one of the first formal documents in the relationship, they can be very telling of what is to come. If I cannot fairly and evenly negotiate an NDA, the likelihood of being able to negotiate a fair contract for the end solution is probably slim.

As you navigate the waters in your own company surrounding NDAs, consider how you approach these – and ensure they are bilateral documents. Avoid the approach many have that their NDAs are not negotiable. In business, everything is negotiable … if you want it to be. And, standing firm on an unbalanced NDA because it's company policy is likely to cost both parties an opportunity.

---

The purpose of a contract should be to govern the relationship and the rules of the program being implemented. And, it should provide a basis of understanding for individuals not previously involved in the business relationship. Sometimes these are broken into separate documents. Some companies will want to have a Master Services Agreement (MSA or Agreement) that governs the terms and conditions of the business relationship. And, then have a separate document, a Statement of Work (SOW) for the details of any individual programs as part of that MSA. Regardless of the approach, the MSA and/or SOW should be written such that anyone not currently involved in the design, selection and implementation of the solution can understand the program and terms of the business relationship.

This is not always easy to do. It requires resources from both parties to take a step back and consider how to write the document as if they don't know anything about the program. This is where the legal staff (contract administrators and attorneys) are excellent resources. The business owners on both sides will often find it difficult to view the language in a way that is anything other than familiar – as if most things could generally be understood.

In negotiating a contract, there is a methodology, or path, I always follow. It begins with a "term sheet" that identifies the business issues to be addressed, followed by a negotiation. Once these are identified and agreed upon, the actual contract can be drafted along with a full legal review. In many organizations, the contract draft and legal review may be the same work effort. The final part of the process is the signatures from both companies which yields the executed agreement.

### Figure 8.1 – Pathway to an Executed Contract

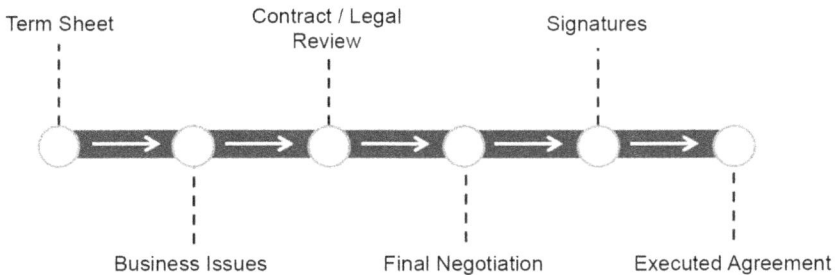

## Term Sheet

Starting with the term sheet is a perfect approach. A term sheet is a document that details the business terms of the deal. If done right, this will include the expectations for both sides. Having the expectations in a brief prior to being inserted in the legal document ensures everyone is in agreement with the business issues. I have learned that nothing frustrates corporate attorneys more than having to review a contract when there are outstanding business issues. It probably doesn't matter who authors the term sheet, but in most deals where I am involved, I usually provide the initial draft. In any case, expect a few iterations before you are actually ready to move into drafting the contract.

Following is an example of an optimal term sheet.

**Figure 8.2 – Sample Term Sheet**

---

### Program Term Sheet for ABC Company
#### Draft #1

- **Term of Agreement** – 5 Years. To be documented in the form of a Master Services Agreement and a Statement of Work, relative to the specific program identified.
- **Program Description** – includes the management and sourcing of the identified solution for ABC Company as documented in the Included Components below. Preferred Provider will manage the delivery of the program objectives, sub-contract vendor relationships, and contracts associated with current and future providers associated with the program. In exchange, Preferred Provider will guarantee committed savings to ABC Company over the five-year term of the Agreement.
- **Included Components:**
  - Marketing communications
  - Corporate identity
  - On-site Print-on-Demand Centers
  - Associated current vendors based on the above categories
- **Excluded Components**
  - Print and mail, except for that which is Direct Mail
  - Envelopes
  - Staffing, except for that which is defined below
- **Enabling Technology** – Certain defined technology will be deployed to the business owners, stakeholders and user community as identified by ABC Company. Based on authority level and designation, components will be made available to ABC Company associates.

---

- **Account Management** – team will include the following:
  - Account Executive – single point of contact for program
  - Account Manager – oversees day-to-day operation
  - Client Care – interfaces with ABC Company business owners and stakeholder
- **Implementation**
  - Key milestone dates
  - Live date of program
  - Gaps to be closed in order to ensure a successful implementation
- **Reporting**
  - Monthly scorecard reporting – Each month, a detailed report will be delivered identifying the progress of the program.
  - Monthly Service Level Agreement reporting – Each month Preferred Provider will provide a scorecard report on the progress during the previous 30 days regarding its performance on meeting certain specific performance objectives.
  - Quarterly review meetings of overall performance – Each quarter, Preferred Provider will have a performance review meeting to review financial and service level commitments.
  - Formal annual business review – Each year ABC Company and Preferred Provider will hold a formal business review of the previous 12 months' performance. This meeting will also be used to identify the go-forward strategy of the Program for both organizations.
- **Program Costs**
  - Program Management
  - Supply Chain Management
  - Enabling Technology
  - Implementation
  - Additional Program Costs
- **Incentives** – Any included financial incentives
- **Additional Program Objectives**

As you review the components of the sample term sheet, you may be thinking that some of these don't apply to your situation. And, that is to be expected. Consider this a guideline of how to construct a document that will work for you and your new partner. The components will be different based on the relationship being formed and the expected solution.

That said, it is worth breaking down the document so you have a deeper understanding of certain components that should be included regardless of the business need.

## Term

The term, or length of the agreement, is fairly straight forward. However, there may be occasions where you want to expand this section. This might include automatic renewals or early termination impacts. When additional circumstances play into the term of the agreement, it is important to have it well documented here.

## Program Description

The program description is one of the most important elements of a term sheet. This should be a fairly specific write-up defining the solution. Consider that this may not be part of the actual contract – but it is important that anyone should be able to read this section and have a good understanding as to what the business need is, and the solution that you are looking to contract.

As an example, let's assume that the attorneys on both sides may not have been intimately involved in crafting the deal. Now, they are being brought in to negotiate the legal terms of a formal agreement. Having a good and reasonably detailed program description will provide the legal staff with enough understanding to begin work. Don't short change this key element.

The placement of the program description immediately underneath the Term is intentional. Within the first two bullet points you will have identified the length of the agreement and what you are trying to solve for.

## Included and Excluded Components

Identifying what is and is not included in the agreement is a critical element to ensuring both parties know what they are about to get themselves into. Often there are assumptions made by one or both parties that may not be fully understood by the other. This is not to suggest there is any underhanded game-playing in the mix. Rather, there may be honest assumptions that neither party ever really thought about disclosing. Or, it could be misinterpretations formed during the selection process.

The included components seem logical – a necessary category that will eventually be added to the contract. But, the excluded components can be a different story. If you think about it, adding components to the agreement that are not part of the program seems unnecessary. And, maybe it is. But, identifying these in the term sheet provides a clear picture to both parties that certain elements are in scope and others are not. Ironing these out before you get to the contract build is important for you and your preferred provider. At this point, the goal is no surprises … for either party!

## Business and Additional Elements

The balance of the term sheet should be used to identify the business elements, and other important topics you will want governed by a contract. These can include technology, account management, implementation, pricing, and any financial incentives. You may also want to include additional information specific to the relationship you are about to enter into.

# Business Issues

If done correctly, the term sheet will have identified all of the business issues for the agreement. This includes certain "non-negotiable" items. This may include intellectual property rights, indemnification, length of agreement, and payment of invoices. There will be terms that seemingly cannot be negotiated (although, I believe most anything is up for negotiation). This is the time to call those out. But, this also means both parties can anticipate a fair amount of negotiations on these and other key points.

Whether through a proposal or an RFP process, there is no way to cover every business issue that may be part of the final agreement. And, even when business issues are addressed in the proposal or RFP response, there may be changes to the final program design. This will inevitably result in new or changed business issues that must be addressed, including pricing.

In an initial proposal, or a response to an RFP, pricing should be considered an estimate of the solution. But, recognize that through better understanding and design of the final solution, the pricing may change. This should not be viewed as an attempt by your partner to change the rules of the game. Rather, it should be considered a more accurate pricing program that represents what you are actually buying as opposed to what was initially presented.

In one of the more complex agreements I worked on, the customer already had a program in place with my company. But, the contract was nearing expiration and they wanted to reshape the program – particularly how the pricing was presented. We provided a detailed proposal in which pricing was a large component.

After we were informed that we were selected to continue the business relationship – but with a new contract, we entered into negotiations. At the beginning of the process the business owner on the customer's side informed us that we were not to change any of the pricing presented in our proposal. That was what I would consider a "guard rail". A guard rail is a certain parameter agreed upon by both parties that provides some guidance on what can and cannot be included in a solution, program or contract. Unfortunately, through several months of discussions, the originally presented pricing was not in either of our best interests. In fact, the customer figured it out before we did. Before the first iteration of the new agreement, they had proposed changes to the pricing. The fact is, their proposed edits were, in concept, very logical. We added some clarifying language and adjusted the pricing to reflect what we believed was their intent – making it financially doable for us.

We ultimately agreed to the language – and the pricing. Later we both chuckled a bit at the emphatic statement that nothing in the pricing section could be altered.

The fact is business issues, including pricing, can and should be negotiated as part of the term sheet. And, neither party should enter the discussions with their heels dug into the sand. Doing so just doesn't help the process.

# The Contract: Legal Review

Once you have completed the term sheet and worked through the business issues, the next step is to ensure legal can agree to the terms in the agreement. I have always found this process to be fascinating. The job of the attorneys is to ensure we do not agree to something that could cause legal harm to either party. As one of our corporate attorneys once told me, "The intention of a contract is to address those unthinkable situations that may just one day present themselves." But, how attorneys talk to each other can be a bit surprising. They can go for the jugular in one breath, and then congratulate each other the very next.

When it's the right time, I like to have a meeting with the attorneys and business owners – from both companies, to address these issues. I find it much easier than continually sending redlined documents back and forth – with the hope that one or both sides will eventually cave on specific issues. But, this occasionally comes with some surprising and spirited conversation between the lawyers.

In one of the larger contracts I negotiated, we reached the point where it was time to invite the attorneys and business owners to a joint conference call. Ironically, both my attorney and that of the client were graduates from the Harvard Law School, although some years apart. Somehow, we got hung up on an issue that seemed unimportant to both myself and my counterpart on the customer's side of the table. But, the attorneys were at each other's throats. At one point, the customer's attorney said, "I have been practicing law for 18 years and I have never seen such an issue or language presented in a contract." My attorney immediately shot back, "Well, I have been practicing for 29 years and if I have learned anything, it is that if we have seen everything there was to see in a contract, neither of us would be necessary, now would we?" At the height of the intensity, I lost it and actually laughed out loud. Admittedly, it was probably not the right time but, neither attorney was fazed by it. Somehow we got through the discussion topic ... but my sponsor and I were both laughing (somewhat nervously) throughout the entire episode.

Regardless of the potential fireworks (which in fairness, do not always occur), it is critically important to engage the lawyers from both sides such that they have a conversation. There are certain legal concerns that only the attorneys can address. This includes things such as limits of liability, intellectual property rights, and indemnification. Rather than going back and forth with redlines – which can significantly drag out the process, have a meeting where all parties can be present and weigh in. In spite of the spirited conversations attorneys can sometimes engage in, I have found them to be highly productive in joint sessions. A discussion with all of the players can go a long way to resolving legal issues in a contract.

# Final negotiation

Inevitably, there will be a final negotiation of specific elements in order to complete an agreement. As I look back on contracts I have worked on, I have come to the conclusion that some of the issues that have become final negotiation points could be considered minor issues. At the time I am sure my customers and I both felt they were huge issues!

The way to approach contract issues is to have the attitude that you are on the home stretch of finalizing the deal. A couple of minor hurdles should not be allowed to derail it!

I recognize that if the negotiation has taken a lengthy amount of time, or the remaining issues are complicated, the final negotiation can be challenging. The best way to manage this is to get all of the parties from both sides, in a room together to go through the remaining issues. This includes the business owners, the attorneys, the sourcing executive or team and the sales executive.

In one of the best-aligned final negotiations I've ever been a part of, the customer put together a meeting to address any remaining issues and finish up the agreement. As we were making the arrangements for the meeting, the customer said, "Let's commit to stay until we come to complete agreement on all remaining issues such that we can quickly move to signature." And, that is what we did.

When we arrived for the meeting at noon, the customer had set up a large conference room and two breakout rooms. The main room was where our joint conversations and negotiations would occur. When necessary for a private discussion, one of the breakout rooms was for the customer, the other was for us. To start the meeting, we went through the MSA and then the SOW. Specifically, we stopped to review and discuss any redlines or comments noted in the documents. Issues that could be addressed in the meeting were negotiated. Certain issues were challenging to decide in the large room, so when necessary, one of the two parties would meet privately and discuss what we could actually agree to. Many issues were tabled, and scheduled for one of two breakout meetings. During the breakouts, we each discussed independently the issues on our list. Then, we reconvened and worked through the remaining issues.

The meeting ended around 7:00 pm, with all open issues negotiated. The final documents were redrafted (redlined), clean copies presented, and we were ready for signatures!

# Signatures

I have often thought at this stage we should have a formal signing event – similar to when the President of the United States signs a bill into law. But, for me this has never happened.

In today's world of electronic communications, it has become generally acceptable that facsimile or electronically scanned copies of signed legal documents are as good as originals. If both parties agree to this, it can certainly speed up the process.

The only goal I have at this point is to quickly secure the signatures so we have an executed agreement and can begin the implementation.

# Executed Agreement

Once the signatures are received – and an "original" is returned to both companies, the deal is done! Much to my surprise, collecting and filing the signed copy with the legal department often becomes a non-event. But, don't let this important step pass you by.

# Statement of Work

In many cases, companies choose to use an SOW to augment an MSA. This may be dependent on the solution, or the approach your company prefers in negotiating agreements. My personal preference is to have the MSA established as a separate document from any SOW.

When an SOW is used, it generally means the MSA contains the legal terms and conditions of the business relationship. With this type of arrangement, the MSA covers things such as contract definitions, invoicing terms, confidentiality, governance, limits of liability, indemnification, intellectual property rights, and licensing. The point is that the MSA can govern the overall relationship while multiple programs can then be deployed as the relationship evolves.

By contrast, an SOW is intended to document the details of a specific program. And, by the terms of the agreement, it almost always becomes an amendment to the MSA. This approach allows you to add multiple programs while knowing you have already agreed to the legal terms in an MSA. Generally, the SOW is negotiated by the line of business, and is subordinate to the MSA. Essentially this means the legal terms in the MSA trumps all.

Using this approach allows the business to add new programs to the partnership without having to spend time negotiating a new contract each time. For this reason, I encourage all of my customers to use this model.

_____

# Key Points

- When you have an incumbent providing a service or product for a sourced need, share your process up front with your current partner.
- Know what it takes to exit existing contracts before you begin a sourcing exercise that may impact a current program.
- Non-Disclosure Agreements (NDAs) are a good practice for all businesses. Ensure ones you enter into are bilateral, equally protecting both parties as you and the provider community exchange information relevant to solving a need.
- A key purpose of the contract is to govern the relationship and terms of a program being implemented. And, it should provide a basis of understanding for individuals not previously involved in the business relationship.
- Many companies refer to the contract as a Master Services Agreement (MSA).
- The pathway to an executed contract should include:
  - Term Sheet
  - Business Issues
  - Contract / Legal Review
  - Final Negotiation
  - Signatures
  - Executed Agreement

- Rather than going back and forth on contract revisions, set up a meeting with the business owners and attorneys from both sides of the table to resolve any open issues.
- Some companies will want to use a Statement of Work (SOW) in addition to a contract. Different than an MSA, an SOW provides details on a specific program that will roll up to the overall Agreement.

# 9

# IMPLEMENTATION

Once you have an optimal solution and selected partner, along with the contract, the next course of business is to implement. Finally! If you are like most companies, it will seem like a lifetime ago that the initiative to find the right solution and partner began – particularly in addressing complex needs. So, arriving at the point of implementation can be a bit of a relief.

At the same time the implementation phase can feel like an insurmountable task that is even more challenging than the sourcing initiative. The feelings will range from questioning if you made the right decision to wondering if the implementation will ever get off the ground. But, you may also experience the satisfaction of the work that got you to this point.

Regardless, as my dad often said, "Get your ducks in a row, it's time to cross the river!" Now is not the time to rest on the laurels of having made a decision. While the momentum is strong, for you and the selected provider, it's time to get started on the implementation. Waiting, even a day, can cause the project to lose steam. And let's face it, at this point both organizations are anticipating the launch.

But, the question remains, "How do I get started?" For a few years I headed up an implementation services organization. This seemed like a logical position for me since I had sold a number of the solutions we had to implement – and for the most part knew what it took to on-board some of the more challenging programs.

Betti Coffey is a well-respected motivational speaker with her own company, Betti Coffey Presents. At one time she was a senior implementation project manager on my team ... and just about one of the best I had the opportunity to work with. In every initial implementation meeting or strategy session on how to begin, Betti would openly discuss what was in store for both organizations. This meant a detailed explanation of the tasks in front of us, and the required resources necessary to pull off the transition. Often it would seem overwhelming. But, at the end she would enthusiastically ask, "So, how does an elephant eat a bushel of apples?" The answer is, "One bite at a time." Regardless of the size or complexity, that is exactly how best to start and accomplish an implementation.

The very first place to begin is in selecting the team, from both organizations, that will guide the implementation. Note the term I used is "team" which is intentionally not plural. At this point, the individuals assigned from both companies have to form a consolidated implementation team. There needs to be a unified focus on implementing the optimal solution. Following is an example of what a project team might look like:

**Figure 9.1 – Example Project Team Chart**

| Your Company | Selected Partner |
|---|---|
| **Project Executive** | **Leadership Executive** |
| **Project Sponsor** | **Sales Executive** |
| **Project Manager** | **Project Manager** |
| Operations | Operations / Manufacturing |
| Finance | Finance |
| Information Technology | Information Technology |
| Line(s) of Business | Professional Services |
| Subject Matter Experts | Subject Matter Experts |

In the above example there are six key positions that are shown in bold. These are the required positions necessary to make most significant or complex implementations successful. For the company, included is the project executive, project sponsor and a project manager. Similarly, the selected partner will have a leadership executive, sales executive and project manager. For the day-to-day activities, the project managers will own the implementation. The project sponsor and sales executive are the "customers" of the project managers. They will guide the project managers so each is aware of the program negotiated and agreed upon. And, the senior executives are in place to clear hurdles, ensure project resources are accessible, and that the overall implementation meets the agreed-upon expectations. Some of these responsibilities may be delegated to the level below them.

The project managers (one for each company) have various team members reporting to them. These are functional reports, and most likely not direct reports. In the example, this includes positions such as operations, finance, IT, lines of business, professional services, and various subject matter experts. The project managers have the primary responsibility to corral the various resources, assign their tasks, and ensure deliverables are met. In addition to the overall management of the on-boarding, the project managers are responsible for reporting to the team and leadership the status of the implementation. There are probably no other positions more critical to the success of the implementation than these two individuals.

Both organizations should provide background information on key members of the implementation team – and in particular the project managers. The background information should include a bio and examples of other, similar projects they have led. In some situations, it may make sense to have a face-to-face meeting with the project managers and the leadership prior to final assignment. It is fair for both companies to know and be comfortable with those who will be leading the initiative.

Once the implementation team is in place, you and your selected partner should spend some time planning how best to tackle the on-boarding. The first step is identifying and documenting the roles and responsibilities of the team members. When you have done this, put them in writing and distribute to everyone involved. Include things as basic as contact information. And, focus more on the functional responsibilities, not individual titles. You are bringing together functional teams from two organizations that likely have never had any formal reporting structure, prior to this engagement. So, this effort will go a long way in establishing the rules of play.

Now that you have the team established, along with roles and responsibilities, it's time to get down to implementing! Start by breaking the implementation into key, yet specific, solution components. Your situation may cause you to approach the implementation differently, such as in phases with components falling up underneath. Regardless, you want to be able to work with your partner to fully understand how the implementation will unfold; both short-term during the on-boarding and then long-term once the program is fully operational.

One of the best visual aids I have used in an initial on-boarding planning session is an implementation plotted graph.

## Figure 9.2 – Implementation Plotted Graph

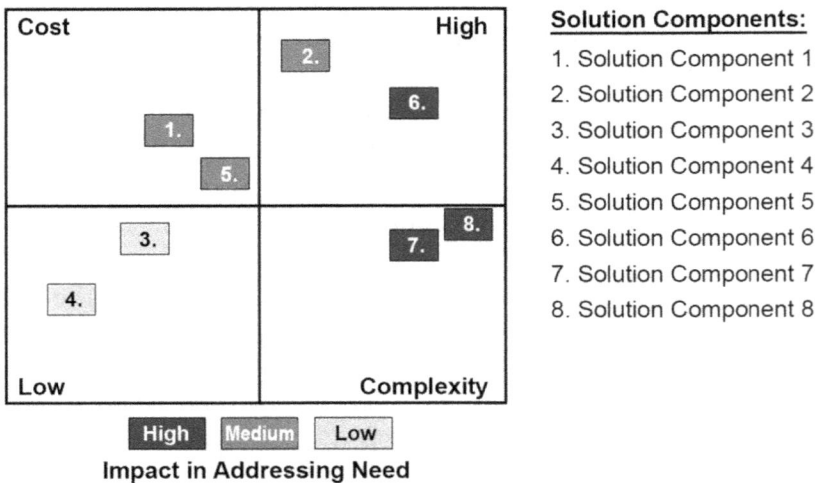

**Solution Components:**

1. Solution Component 1
2. Solution Component 2
3. Solution Component 3
4. Solution Component 4
5. Solution Component 5
6. Solution Component 6
7. Solution Component 7
8. Solution Component 8

You will see the graph has four quadrants that compare the identified solution categories, from complexity to cost. Low cost, low complexity will be in the lower left quadrant, whereas high cost, high complexity will be in the upper right quadrant. Then, each solution component is weighted in terms of its importance to impacting or solving the need.

Spending the time to plot the solution components will give you and your selected partner a better understanding of the options in front of you. Through this process you may notice that some of the lower cost items can actually yield a bigger impact to your project. And, the more complex solutions are not always the most costly to implement. This visual exercise can be enlightening on many fronts in terms of where to start the process. Once completed, the graph will provide the framework to determine the sequence of events for the implementation. Sometimes less complex components that may not always yield the highest impact are good places to start. This allows you to build some proof cases and create momentum before tackling more complex components.

One of the early risk factors you want to avoid is choosing to bite off more than you can chew (remember the elephant and bushel of apples). This may ultimately create an outward view that the project is unsuccessful, before it is even fully implemented. If opinions start forming early in the implementation that a project is not going well, it can be difficult for you and your partner to regain support the solution may need long-term. Together you and your selected partner can make the best determination for your specific situation.

# The Project Plan

The project managers are now ready to build an implementation project plan containing the detailed requirements of the solution. There are a variety of different project plan types you can consider. But, the Gantt chart is one of the most widely accepted tools and provides the best visual aid to work with.

When creating a Gantt chart, you can use Excel® or programs such as Microsoft® Project (MS Project) that are specifically designed for project management. The more sophisticated you want to get, the more you will want to consider a tool such as MS Project. Most skilled project managers usually use this as their tool of choice. But, don't worry if you don't have the software. They can output it as a PDF.

The Gantt chart should be considered a living document and tool, and not something created at the start of the implementation never to be touched again. Issues will arise and new learnings will come about that will alter the detail of the project plan as you move forward. This is ok. But, keeping these changes documented in the project plan will allow you and others on the team to see the impact of missed deadlines, discovered learnings, or the addition of new tasks. It will even show you the positive effect of finishing milestones ahead of schedule.

When using advanced toolsets like MS Project, there are a number of different ways you can create a Gantt chart. Every situation may yield a different view – and preferences from one provider to another will invariably influence the fields you see in a plan. However, there are some basic guidelines worth sharing that every Gantt chart should contain.

The example chart in Figure 9.3 contains what I believe are the minimum required fields in any implementation – regardless of size or scope. The first column contains WBS, or Work Breakdown Structure. This creates an outline numbering system so you can easily see the tasks that fall under other categories. It also makes the hierarchy of the plan easy to understand. This is followed by the percentage of completion and task description. The description should clearly identify the work to be done, but not be overly verbose. Real estate is precious in a Gantt chart. The next three columns deal with the amount of time it takes to complete a task. You will see the number of days to completion, along with start and finish dates. If you are not familiar with a Gantt chart, predecessors can be a confusing category. This ties a specific task to another task (its predecessor) that should be completed or at least started before the task in review can begin. Finally, and probably one of the more important columns is the resource names. You will notice in the example project plan there are very specific names associated with each task. This is because people actually make sure that tasks get accomplished. Unfortunately, titles alone do not equate to accountability. Thus, be certain to ensure individual names are assigned to each task. You will be amazed at how well tasks get accomplished when an individual is named.

### Figure 9.3 – Sample Project Plan

| | | | Strategic Solution Implementation Plan Draft # 1 | | | | | |
|---|---|---|---|---|---|---|---|---|
| ID | WBS | % Complete | Task Name | Duration | Start | Finish | Predecessors | Resource Names |
| 0 | 0 | 0% | **Strategic Solution Implementation Plan** | 67.06 days | Thu 12/1/16 | Mon 3/6/17 | | |
| 1 | 1 | 0% | **Pre-Implementation Planning** | 11.5 days | Thu 12/1/16 | Fri 12/16/16 | | **Thomas R,Jones T** |
| 2 | 1.1 | 0% | **Pre-Implementation Scoping Meeting** | 1 day | Thu 12/1/16 | Thu 12/1/16 | | **Thomas R,Jones T** |
| 3 | 1.1.1 | 0% | Review Pre-Implementation Survey to determine project scope | 1 day | Thu 12/1/16 | Thu 12/1/16 | | Jenkins R,Smith S |
| 4 | 1.1.2 | 0% | Confirm LOI is signed, project scoped | 1 day | Thu 12/1/16 | Thu 12/1/16 | | Jenkins R |
| 5 | 1.1.3 | 0% | Review contract terms and conditions | 1 day | Thu 12/1/16 | Thu 12/1/16 | | Smith S,Jenkins R |
| 6 | 1.2 | 0% | Assign Project Team | 0.5 days | Fri 12/2/16 | Fri 12/2/16 | 2 | Thomas R,Jones T |
| 7 | 1.3 | 0% | Establish Roles and Responsibilities of Project Team | 2 days | Fri 12/2/16 | Tue 12/6/16 | 6 | Thomas R,Jones T |
| 8 | 1.4 | 0% | Identify and Define Project Solution Categories | 8 days | Tue 12/6/16 | Fri 12/16/16 | 2,6,7 | Thomas R,Jones T |
| 9 | 1.5 | 0% | **Preferred Partner Internal Kick-off Meeting** | 1 day | Fri 12/2/16 | Fri 12/2/16 | 2 | Davidson J |
| 15 | 1.6 | 0% | Develop preliminary Gantt chart | 5 days | Fri 12/2/16 | Thu 12/8/16 | 2 | Thomas R |
| 16 | 2 | 0% | **Customer Preliminary Conference Calls** | 3 days | Mon 12/5/16 | Wed 12/7/16 | 9 | **Jones T** |
| 17 | 2.1 | 0% | Review Legal Agreement | 1 day | Mon 12/5/16 | Mon 12/5/16 | | Bush H,Douglas L |
| 18 | 2.2 | 0% | Confirm targeted live date | 2 days | Tue 12/6/16 | Wed 12/7/16 | 17 | Douglas L,Bush H |
| 19 | 2.3 | 0% | **Request customer information** | 0.13 days | Mon 12/5/16 | Mon 12/5/16 | | **Sams S** |
| 28 | 2.4 | 0% | Develop and discuss escalation plan | 1 day | Mon 12/5/16 | Mon 12/5/16 | | Douglas L,Bush H |
| 29 | 2.5 | 0% | Set schedule for future calls | 1 day | Mon 12/5/16 | Mon 12/5/16 | | Jones T,Thomas R |
| 30 | 2.6 | 0% | **Set schedule for Client kickoff** | 2 days | Tue 12/6/16 | Wed 12/7/16 | 29 | **Thomas R,Jones T** |
| 31 | 2.6.1 | 0% | Confirm agenda items and availability of client resources | 1 day | Tue 12/6/16 | Tue 12/6/16 | | Jones T,Thomas R |
| 32 | 2.6.2 | 0% | Confirm location; timeframe; on-site/conference call requirements | 1 day | Wed 12/7/16 | Wed 12/7/16 | 31 | Jones T,Thomas R |

By now the question has probably entered your mind, "Who actually owns the project plan?" Well, the answer comes down to the project manager for either your company or the selected partner. In most cases, I believe the project manager for the selected partner is the ideal resource to own the project plan. They are going to know best what it takes to implement the optimal solution. This doesn't mean your project manager is off the hook. It only refers to the fact that the partner's project manager is the gatekeeper of the document, and is responsible for maintaining the updates to the project plan. Your project manager will need to continue owning tasks, resources and deliverables on your side to ensure deadlines are met.

# Maintaining Progress of the Implementation

Since the Gantt chart is intended to be not only an initial planning document, but a tool to help throughout the implementation process, maintaining the progress is an essential element. This means providing on-going updates to the Gantt chart, recording notes and other relevant information, and holding status meetings for the team. In addition, periodic updates for the executives on both sides of the table are important throughout the implementation.

## Gantt Chart: A Living and Breathing Document

Regardless of the complexity of the implementation, I have found that weekly updates to the Gantt chart is the right frequency. This provides a living and breathing toolset for the benefit of those involved with the implementation. It also ensures executives can have a view of the status – at a higher level.

Gantt chart updates should be done well in advance of any status or review meeting. This allows those who have deliverables to review the tasks and ensure the information is captured correctly. It also provides the resources with what is expected that week and beyond. And, it delivers a glaring visual for those tasks that were completed late or missed entirely.

Earlier we covered the importance of including very specific names under resources. The weekly update is where this becomes highly effective. After the first couple of review meetings, resources will become very accustomed to opening the weekly Gant Chart and searching for their names. Each will be looking for two things:

1. Where does my name appear, and what are the associated tasks?
2. What expected deliverables did I miss or deliver late?

It won't take long before missed deliverables become an eyesore with which most resources will want to ensure their names are not associated.

## Implementation Notes

Depending on the implementation, often driven by complexity, the updated Gantt chart alone may not be sufficient to capture all that is going on with the project. In these situations, implementation notes may be used to augment the updated Gantt chart. However, this does not mean that notes can replace the Gantt chart.

When implementation notes become necessary, these should be provided weekly – and contain only information currently relevant. This may include specific information about tasks that are due. Or, it may be related to key issues that could be impacting the deliverables – and ultimately any planned live date. As with the Gantt chart, specific resource names, dates of the activity, and required actions are important to include.

In one of my first large scale implementations, it became evident the Gantt chart alone would not be sufficient to cover the level of detail involved. Specifically, some of the unexpected issues that cropped up during the process were not being captured. The executive sponsor from the customer asked to see me about his concerns on this matter.

During the meeting, the executive sponsor and I agreed that we would begin recording – in a separate document to augment the Gantt chart, specific notes related to deliverables of the project. He requested this be titled, "Transition, Quality and Sloppiness." Each part of the heading would become its own category in the notes document.

Transition would deal with those areas requiring additional information on the shift from the current state as documented in the Gantt chart – and relevant for that specific week. Quality would be those items where top quality and above-performance was worth noting. This would be used to spotlight those resources that were doing an excellent job. The final category, Sloppiness, would be used to focus on areas where the team was dropping the ball.

Through several conversations over a period of a few days, the executive sponsor and I discussed that last category. I could not get past the awful connotation "Sloppiness" had, and the effect it would have on the team. That effect, however, is exactly what the executive sponsor wanted. He believed that if we blatantly called out sloppiness then people would react, and avoidable issues would begin to disappear. I ultimately lost that plea – the title of the report stood as "Transition, Quality and Sloppiness."

It is important to note that sloppiness issues were on both sides. And, although there were not very many – they were usually fairly ugly. But, the executive sponsor was right. After a few weeks, the Sloppiness category had dwindled to a point where I wondered if we really needed it anymore. When I realized I would have to gain the support of the executive sponsor to remove the category, the thought quickly passed. It stayed until the end of the implementation.

As hard as this is for me to admit, the "Transition, Quality and Sloppiness" report proved to be a valuable tool to augment the Gantt chart. The implementation was complex enough that the Gantt chart alone did not suffice.

Regardless of the document's title, you may find that recording weekly status notes can be an important addition to the process. The key leaders of the implementation team can help make the decision that is right for you.

## Weekly Status Meetings

Weekly meetings to review the status of the implementation are extremely important – in fact as much as the Gantt chart. The first few sessions may seem a bit long. But, in short order these should be limited to no more than one hour. The goal is to review the status, point out any issues that need to be dealt with, and redirect to off-line discussions where necessary.

Some may argue that this is nothing more than a rehash of what is in the Gantt chart and notes. And, maybe it is. But, I have found that when the resources have to answer to the project managers in front of their peers – it can be highly motivating to ensure deliverables are met. Maybe in the beginning this doesn't occur that smoothly … but after having to answer to missed deliverables a couple of times, I suspect you will soon find a change in behavior.

Kenneth P. Davis, PhD., worked for the US government in a civil service position where he headed up a large team and segment of logistics for the military. He and I are active volunteers at a national level in the Boy Scouts of America®. For a number of years, I worked for Ken in a group that provided administrative services for large-scale national scout conferences. When I first started working for him, I was still in college but, quickly learned Ken was a master at running meetings – and keeping them to a manageable timeframe.

Ken would start every review meeting promptly. And, within one hour we were done. Although he never said it, I suspect he believed that what we couldn't accomplish in an hour just wasn't going to get done in that meeting. So, he would ask each individual to give a report out. He generally had a couple of key questions for each of us. And, if anyone got too deep in their report out, Ken would cut off the discussion. Often he would suggest certain individuals work offline to resolve an issue, and report back to him. Or, he might ask one or more of us to get with him after the meeting. It got to be a challenge for me to see if I could get through my report out without being cut off – while still answering any question he pitched my way.

That was one of the first leadership lessons that I integrated into my professional life. I began using that same approach in internal and customer meetings. To this day, I still run sessions exactly like Ken. Relative to implementations this means a quick review of deliverables due, report outs from key resources, and redirects for issues that are too involved to resolve in the allotted one hour. Your project managers should strive to do the same thing. It will prove to be highly effective.

## Executive Dashboard

It is unlikely that the executives of either organization will regularly attend the weekly implementation status meetings. Perhaps one or both will show up on occasion, but weekly attendance is probably out of the question. And, if the implementation team is doing its job, this level of executive involvement should not be necessary.

This does not mean, however, that it isn't important to keep the executives from both companies informed. I have found that an executive dashboard is an excellent approach. Following is an example of an effective executive dashboard:

### Figure 9.4 – Executive Dashboard

Executive Management Project Dashboard

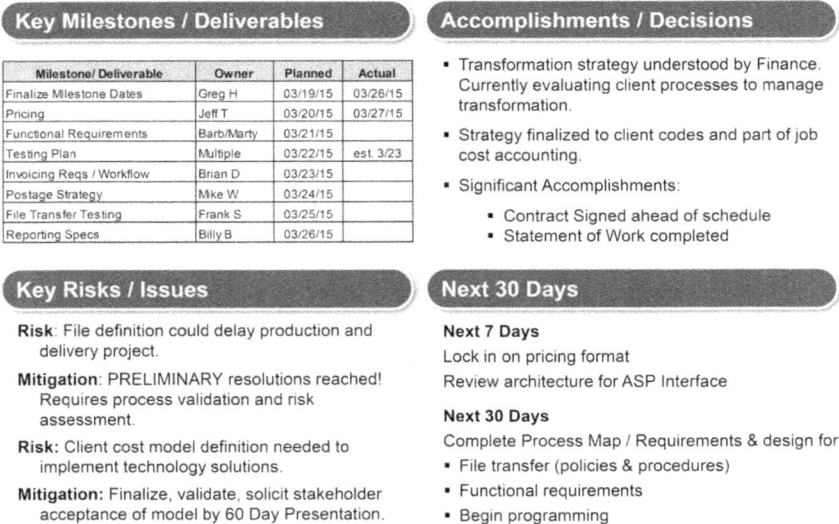

**Key Milestones / Deliverables**

| Milestone/ Deliverable | Owner | Planned | Actual |
|---|---|---|---|
| Finalize Milestone Dates | Greg H | 03/19/15 | 03/26/15 |
| Pricing | Jeff T | 03/20/15 | 03/27/15 |
| Functional Requirements | Barb/Marty | 03/21/15 | |
| Testing Plan | Multiple | 03/22/15 | est. 3/23 |
| Invoicing Reqs / Workflow | Brian D | 03/23/15 | |
| Postage Strategy | Mike W | 03/24/15 | |
| File Transfer Testing | Frank S | 03/25/15 | |
| Reporting Specs | Billy B | 03/26/15 | |

**Accomplishments / Decisions**

- Transformation strategy understood by Finance. Currently evaluating client processes to manage transformation.
- Strategy finalized to client codes and part of job cost accounting.
- Significant Accomplishments:
  - Contract Signed ahead of schedule
  - Statement of Work completed

**Key Risks / Issues**

**Risk**: File definition could delay production and delivery project.

**Mitigation**: PRELIMINARY resolutions reached! Requires process validation and risk assessment.

**Risk:** Client cost model definition needed to implement technology solutions.

**Mitigation:** Finalize, validate, solicit stakeholder acceptance of model by 60 Day Presentation.

**Next 30 Days**

**Next 7 Days**
Lock in on pricing format
Review architecture for ASP Interface

**Next 30 Days**
Complete Process Map / Requirements & design for:
- File transfer (policies & procedures)
- Functional requirements
- Begin programming

The Executive Dashboard has four quadrants: key milestone deliverables, critical accomplishments, key risks and issues, and next 30 days.

## Key Milestones

Key Milestones is a roll-up from the detail in the Gantt chart. It provides the executives with a quick glance at the progression of the project, avoiding the need to sift through the detail of the entire project plan.

## Critical Accomplishments

Critical Accomplishments highlights success stories or critical events that have impacted the implementation in a positive manner. Often we tend to focus on the problem areas. Not to make light of issues and concerns, but it is equally important to recognize things going well.

## Key Risks and Issues

Key Risks and Issues are those elements that, if not addressed, could derail the implementation. Sometimes there may be a mitigation plan already in play – or a recommendation to correct the issue. Use this section to briefly highlight items that could have a significant impact to the implementation.

## Next 30 Days

The Next 30 Days is an opportunity to look at what's ahead. Understanding what has been accomplished is valuable information – but until the implementation is completed, knowing what lies ahead is equally important.

# What Went Wrong?

Occasionally the pop and sizzle of a selected solution and partner fade during the implementation. As a result, I have witnessed my fair share of challenging or failed implementations. Most can be attributed to one of the following issues:

1. Lack of executive sponsorship from either the company, the partner, or both;
2. Limited time and resources from the company buying the solution to invest in implementing;
3. Lack of complete understanding of the current state and the need;
4. Oversold solution or wrong provider selected that cannot fully address the need;
5. Weak implementation team.

## Lack of Sponsorship

Just as the sourcing initiative requires sponsorship and executive buy-in, so does the implementation. In fact, some may argue that executive support is more important during the implementation than any other part of the process. In the end, it will not serve anyone well if you select a great strategy and partner, but the solution cannot be effectively implemented.

The largest reason I see for challenging or failed implementations is the lack of sponsorship from one or both companies. Depending on the significance of the initiative, the sponsorship from an executive level is imperative to ensure success. For this reason, sponsorship needs to be secured early in the process – well in advance of getting to the point of implementation. Consider garnering this level of support from your company at the point you decide to source the need. If you can't get it, then reconsider continuing with the project. Likewise, when you identify potential providers, ensure you are having conversations with the executives to enlist their support of the implementation once a decision is made.

## Limited Time and Resources

Limited time and resources can be one of the more challenging obstacles to overcome in a difficult or failing implementation. Often, the very need that drove the search for a solution is tied to lack of time and resources. Trying to solve for this problem without them creates a vicious cycle you just cannot seem to get out of.

While one option may be to abandon the project, I would encourage you to first look for a solution to address the gap. Only use abandonment as a last resort. There are a couple of things that I have seen help when limited time and resources present themselves as significant issues.

First, share with your newly selected partner – full disclosure – what is going on. Many solution providers have additional resources they can make available to help close gaps on your side. Certainly this cannot address every gap, but there are likely a number of things your partner can bring to the table – above and beyond what you may have contracted with them to do. Depending on the need, this may come at a slight incremental cost. But, that may be better than bailing on the implementation. In addition, your selected partner may have seen this exact situation before. Oftentimes it may feel as if you are the only one facing certain issues, when in reality many other companies have similar experiences. Use your partner's expertise to learn how the other companies solved for the issue.

Second, escalate to the executive sponsor of the project. At this stage of solving for the need, most will not want to see the project die on the vine. It's worth mentioning again that the earlier you secure executive support, the easier this conversation will be when needed.

## Lack of Current State Understanding and Need

There will be times when the current state assessment looks great on paper, and both parties believe there is a solid understanding of the need. Yet, it becomes apparent there are significant disconnects when it's time to implement the solution. This is when I see the "blame game" come out in full force. It generally sounds something like, "How could you not know? We explained this in detail to you throughout the process and in our discussions?" While there can be legitimate blame on one or both sides, that's probably not going to accomplish much at this point.

There are really two options:

1. Go back and re-define the current state, and potentially the solution.
2. Separate from the partner you have selected.

Option 2 may end up being the best choice. But, before you jump to conclusions, consider that option 1 is worth investing some time in. I have found when both parties go back and redefine the current state – with an open mind, it can often lead to a better understanding and a tweaking of the solution, allowing you to get back to the implementation. Hard as it may be, both parties need to shelve the grumbling and spend some time on this. When I have participated in implementations where reigniting the current state assessment and solution build has occurred, it resulted in a stronger understanding of the current state and a more viable solution. And, most were back on track in a short period of time.

## Oversold Solution / Wrong Provider Selected

When an implementation is struggling to get off the ground, or maybe even failing, I see emotions of the project team ranging from disappointment, to fear of having selected the wrong provider, to complete disgust and irritation. Regardless, at some point in your sourcing career the selection of a wrong provider is going to happen. Sometimes this is due to an oversold solution. This generally becomes obvious when you are trying to get the implementation off the ground. The test of how a project team reacts is not in defending a bad selection, but how quickly it can change course when needed.

I worked with an international financial services firm that focused on institutions, corporations and high-net worth individuals. Their sourcing objective was to find a solution that would consolidate and more effectively manage the procurement of their marketing communications. The process began with a product-based RFP – the type I would not ordinarily respond to. But, because my company was one of a number of incumbents invited to participate, we presented a proposal. With the response, we provided an alternative strategy that focused on managing all of the communications in a holistic outsourced program. This was a radical shift, as the management of the current-state program was being handled by 14 different brands who independently bought their own materials. On top of this, there was a corporate marketing group who had a separate program in place.

The consolidated program we recommended in the alternative strategy caught the attention of the project team, particularly the project sponsor. After a number of meetings, and a good bit of time, the project sponsor decided to abandon the RFP and move in the direction of our recommended strategy. But, the sponsor was honest and advised us that one of our competitors would also be invited to participate. We were each asked to perform a current state assessment and develop a recommended solution.

We worked diligently on our proposed solution, and knew we had very good alignment with the sourcing team – as the recommended approach was ours to begin with. What we did not expect is the competitor had business in other parts of the organization, unrelated to this initiative, and that they would use it to leverage this deal. By contrast, the only business we had was directly related to this particular need. Our competitor used their leverage to tie into senior executives of the firm who ultimately decided to select them as the go-forward provider.

The selection of our competitor was not solely on relationship, however. They offered the firm incredible incentives, and what on paper appeared to be an amazing recommended solution. To the firm, it seemed like an obvious choice.

As disappointed as we were, we stayed in contact with the firm and performed a debrief. They were incredibly supportive of our requests to stay in contact – and accepted every invitation we had to talk or meet. And, were very open about the selection process, and why they chose the route they did.

Late one Friday night after the implementation was underway, the firm's project sponsor called us with a rather surprising request. He asked if we would consider coming back for further discussions of our proposal and offer. It turned out our competitor had never actually managed a complete outsourced program in this space. It became evident when they met with various lines of business and the marketing group. There was no level of subject matter expertise and there was a lack of organization around the implementation. As a result, the selected partner was losing support from the lines of business. Without their support, the project was doomed.

We immediately re-engaged and picked up where we left off. The competitor was dismissed from the project and we were awarded the business. Today the program is fully implemented yielding excellent results – better than anticipated. The customer and the lines of business are happy with the final outcome – and so am I.

The underlying message of this story is that the project team and my team both had back-up plans if the initially selected company failed. We quickly engaged and continued on with very little disruption to the project. As much as you may believe you have selected the right solution and partner, stay in contact with your other options. You never know when you may need them.

## Weak Implementation Team

Depending on the organization, on either side of the table, a weak implementation team can stall or derail the project. I have seen every imaginable scenario, including weak project managers, insufficiently trained subject matter experts, and executive sponsors who are missing in action.

As with many of the points above, the right approach is to address the problem head on with your partner – and without blame. Identify the issues, involve the right resources to address, and fix them! While there may be times where situations are just not fixable, many are. The partnership which you so diligently formed will be instrumental in addressing a weak implementation team. Use that to the advantage of you and your selected go-forward partner.

---

Keeping the right mindset during the implementation will help determine its outcome. Recognize that there is no perfect implementation – regardless of what you may have perceived during the solution identification and partner selection process. If there is, I have never been part of one. You may have even spoken to references that provided glowing remarks on their own implementation. But, the nature of the beast is you will likely experience bumps in the road. Since there is no way to document everything there is to know in the current state or the recommended solution, learnings will continue through the implementation period. This is part of the process.

If you and your selected partner go into the implementation with this in mind, you will have the wherewithal and flexibility to adjust based on unexpected situations and new learnings as they pop up. This is not the time to blame others, or in a worst case scenario throw in the towel.

---

# Key Points

- The first place to start in an implementation is selecting the team from both companies.
- Document the various roles and responsibilities of each implementation team member.
- Determine the order in which you want to tackle the various components of the implementation. This should be done in concert with the company and go-forward partner.
- Develop a detailed project plan that will guide you through the process. A Gantt chart is an ideal tool to consider. Ensure the project plan is a living document that is regularly reviewed and updated throughout the process.

- Implementation notes can be used to augment the project plan during weekly or regularly scheduled status update meetings.
- Consider using an executive dashboard to keep executives informed as to the status of the implementation. This is a one-page report that executives can quickly review and determine the status of the project.
- Poor implementations can often be attributed to one of the following issues:
  - Lack of executive sponsorship
  - Limited time and resources
  - Lack of understanding of the current state and need
  - Oversold solution
  - Weak implementation team

  Since it has likely taken a long time to get to the point of implementation, work to resolve any issues and move on. This is not the time to throw in the towel!
- There is no perfect implementation! Know there will be bumps in the road. How you react to those bumps can be the difference between a successful or failed implementation.

# 10

# THE SOURCING EXECUTIVE
# &
# SALES EXECUTIVE

In any buying and selling activity, the relationship between the sourcing executive and sales executive can heavily influence the outcome of the go-forward solution. Regardless of what the textbooks say, people do business with people they like to work with. And, many will go out of their way to protect that approach.

This goes deeper than we often think. No matter the product or solution I may offer – at the end of the day it is only people who make business work. At one time I worked for a vice president of sales who used to say, "Our greatest asset is our people." He genuinely believed that regardless of the products or services we provided, how our associates performed and the professional relationships they built mattered most. And, although we are talking about the relationship between the sales executive and sourcing executive, he extended this well beyond these two roles. He believed relationships at all levels were the only true differentiator among providers. This includes sales, customer service, operations, implementation, finance, IT, and more.

As a result, I took to heart early in my career that the relationship I build with prospective customers matters as much as the recommended solution I may pitch. We all like to think that a purely objective and measureable approach is the only way to select the right solution and optimal business partner. However, if the sales executive and sourcing executive or their respective teams haven't built any kind of professional business relationship, the best solution most likely will not be selected. This is not to suggest that the substance of the solution is immaterial. Rather, it is to point out that a mutual respect for the professionals involved in the potential partnership is worth a lot more than most want to admit. And, the business relationship formed between the two executives can actually help form a solid foundation of ensuring that a great solution is formulated and then implemented between the two companies.

During my role leading an implementation organization I was working to on-board a national insurance company in the Midwest. This was a Business Process Outsourcing (BPO) initiative where my company was selected as the go-forward partner.

This particular initiative was being led by an outside consulting firm the insurance company had retained. Through the selling process and implementation, I built a great relationship with the consulting firm and the sourcing team. Most of this was the result of my team and me working diligently to understand the business requirements, build out the specifics of the solution, and then successfully implement the optimal program. It was easy to form and continue to build the relationship because we spent so much time together throughout the process. In fact, the two consultants and I often stayed at the same hotel and would have an occasional drink after a number of long days.

One of the implementation tasks was to assign the account management team from my company that would own the business relationship once the sales and implementation folks were out of the picture. As is typical for an opportunity that size and complexity, we hired an experienced account manager from inside our company. And, the customer had a chance to meet and interview the manager before the assignment was made. The consultants also met and interviewed our candidate. In the end, the decision was made – and the account manager was put in place.

Soon after the formal assignment, the account manager began work. He showed up to the client site every day – and worked alongside the implementation team learning the nuances of the program, and helping us get it off the ground. He took it upon himself to get to know the company's business executives and began building relationships with them. That was as designed – and an important part of the sales and implementation teams being able to successfully move on once our jobs were done.

During a casual encounter after work at the hotel, the two consultants approached me with some concerns about the account manager. While he was a likeable guy, it seemed he was pressuring the senior business executive to play a round of golf at one of the country clubs where he was a member. This wasn't all that unusual but, what made it odd is this was the sole focus of his conversations – and seemed to be persistent day after day. The customer was becoming irritated – and ultimately asked that we find another account manager. That's kind of a drastic move. But, I appreciated the fact I had a solid enough relationship with the customer and the consultants that they would directly share the concern.

Knowing that the relationship between the account manager and the business executive was essential to making the solution a success, we made the tough decision to find another account manager. This was not done lightly – we did explore the possibility of corrective action to help the account manager better interact with the executives of his new customer. After much discussion, internally and with the customer, we decided that trying to change the behavior of our account manager just wasn't going to fix the problem. In the end the right resolution was a new manager. Once in place he and the business executives hit it off very well. And, the new program was seamlessly transitioned from the sales and implementation teams to the account management team. The relationship the account manager and senior executive built early in the process, and even more so after we were gone, allowed for further enhancements to the program. To the benefits of both companies, the new account manager developed a strong partnership that lasted for many years.

Since the relationship between the sourcing executive and the sales executive is essential, it is worth reviewing some of the personality types of each that can contribute to, or inhibit, achieving the goal of identifying the best solution and partner.

# The Sourcing Executive

As a sales executive, I have worked with sourcing executives in every realm imaginable, including the pushover, strategic thinker, VIP, and hard ass. Depending on the need and sourcing activity, each can play a different role. In building a professional relationship there are pros and cons to most of these.

## The Pushover

I have to admit; this is one I don't see very often. But, every now and then I run into a pushover. This is an individual that provides little direction, and just wants a solution to the problem – without much interaction. Often this individual has more on their plate than they know what to do with. And, addressing the specific need is just one more thing to be dealt with.

Sometimes there is an advantage to this kind of resource. It allows the sales executive and team a great deal of autonomy to develop one or more solutions that have few guard rails. Then, the business owner or team can pick and choose. This assumes, though, that the decision making process is relatively easy. In other words, the options are not so confusing or complicated that making a selection becomes more time consuming than if the sourcing executive were more engaged from the start.

The downside is it may become difficult to gain a full and accurate understanding of the need. Incoming information regarding the current state may be vague, or understated. As a result, the solution may not be the right fit. Then, during implementation issues can start rising to the surface.

## Strategic Thinker

I find the strategic thinker to be the most enjoyable sourcing executive to work with. This individual digs deeply into the strategy of their company, how the specific need connects to that strategy, and then searches for a solution that is equally strategic. It generally involves searching for a solution that carries an ROI and benefit for the business as opposed to a cost only play.

The strategic thinker is generally well thought of in their own organization. This translates into the sourcing team having a great deal of respect for the strategic thinker. As a result, they are able to engage the right resources because they just want to work on a team that is strategic. If you think about it, most of us enjoy strategic solution development over repetitive tasks or activities where we just don't stretch our minds.

When married up with a strategic team from the potential providers, this resource can become the best bridge to finding the right solution and go-forward partner. There is no doubt that the strategic thinker has the best shot at achieving the right sourcing solution for an identified need.

## VIP

A VIP is a sourcing executive that views themselves as one of the most important people on earth. Because of a sizeable ego, the worst part is they probably don't even realize it. Often VIPs will want to take the stage and opine on how important they and the initiative are. This may be accompanied by further discussion on how busy they are, and the various meetings with senior executives they will be attending.

A VIP can be an inhibiter ... but, almost never intentionally. A significant amount of otherwise productive time might be spent pontificating rather than digging into the details of a need and potential solution.

On the other hand, a VIP can open doors that provides both the organization and the potential providers access to individuals who understand the current state business. They can also become the conduit to ensure the right individuals are engaged to evaluate a recommended solution. For this reason, a VIP is my second favorite sourcing executive.

## Hard Ass

A hard ass is the individual who likes to exert an authority level and "toughness" toward the sales executive. This includes asking the sales executive to jump through unnecessary hoops on ridiculous timetables, an aggressive tone when negotiating, and a general sense the sales executive is a complete bother.

When I began my professional selling career, this was the way many sourcing executives operated. It was a rite of passage for the new sales executive to break through the barrier of a seasoned sourcing executive such that they would actually entertain a discussion on a solution. I would have thought by now these personalities would be extinct in the sourcing world. Surprisingly, there are a number of sourcing executives that still fall into this category.

In my very first role as a sales executive I was calling on an architectural firm. The sourcing executive was an existing customer of my company – but I was new to the relationship. I called and asked for a first meeting and we set an appointment for the following week. I arrived promptly on time, and his assistant escorted me up to his office. The office had a glass wall across the front and his name on the door. The assistant directed me to a small lobby directly outside of his office and advised the sourcing executive would be with me shortly. I could tell there was no one else in the sourcing executive's office but him, and he was not on the phone. However, he appeared to be busy reading and shuffling papers. After about 15 minutes, he came out to get me. We went in his office, and I'm sure I had a look of surprise on my face, if not complete disbelief. His desk, guest chairs, and floor were covered in stacks of papers. Some were so tall I don't know how he kept them from toppling over. Not only was there nowhere to sit, there was hardly any place to stand. Finally, he spoke, "You know why there's no place to sit? It's because I don't want sales reps hanging around here!" My first encounter with a hard ass.

The problem with a hard ass is they inhibit the selling process. But, equally important they impact the buying process. When I first started selling, I had little option but to suck it up and take whatever abuse came down the pike from a hard ass. But, I no longer do that. And, most seasoned sales executives will draw a line on accepting this kind of approach. This extends well beyond just the sales executive, too. I have seen situations where a potential provider will refuse to work with some companies simply because of how they treat sales executives and other associates.

The net effect of hard asses is they cause potential misses on solutions that may actually help the companies. If sales executives or potential providers withdraw because of challenges in dealing with a customer, everyone loses out on what could be the best possible solution.

I wish I could tell you there is an upside to being a hard ass. But frankly, I can't think of one.

# The Sales Executive

As with sourcing executives, sales executives come in a few different shapes and sizes. And, I have come across or worked with most of them. The personality types of a sales executive include the good ole' boy, rapid closer, never ending talker, empathizer, creative thinker, and strategist.

## Good Ole' Boy

The good ole' boy is a bit old school. But, surprisingly this sales executive is still an active player in the business world. Generally, he likes to schmooze or wine and dine the sourcing executive and sourcing team. This is his primary approach to conveying the optimal solution for a specific need.

I suspect you may be wondering how effective this can really be. Although this is not generally consistent with my own personal style, it can actually work fairly well. A good ole' boy has the ability to convey the optimal solution in an environment that can be very comfortable for the sourcing executive. Sometimes getting out of the office to have a business discussion surrounding a specific need can be productive to identifying the best possible solution. Through a casual conversation it can also result in some creative solutions that just cannot be developed in a fixed appointment time at the office.

This is not to suggest that there is no substance to the solution development. It's just a different approach – with a venue that challenges the traditional office environment. These venues can include business dinners, golf outings, or even business trips that involve production or manufacturing facilities.

You can likely see the downside to this approach. In today's business environment, the good ole' boy presents certain ethical challenges that even five or ten years ago just didn't exist. In fact, when I first started professional selling, this was a very common practice. As businesses strive to create a fair and evenly competitive environment, handling business activities in social settings is being challenged more than ever. And frankly, I have seen deals brokered over expensive dinners where I knew it was just not the best way to select a partner. The challenge with this approach is to be able to identify the best possible solution without a bias that can warp the decision making process.

## Rapid Closer

If you have been in the sourcing world for any period of time, then you have likely encountered a rapid closer. The rapid closer is the individual who just wants to close the deal. This can even be at the expense of the right solution. If there is a close in sight, then who really cares if the solution hits the mark? The rapid closer is often looking to cash in on the quick sale.

But, before you write this one off completely – consider the potential upside. A rapid closer can actually help you identify the right solution in a quick timeframe. If the sales executive is motivated to close a deal, they may actually work diligently to provide the right solution more quickly than the executive who has other pending deals. And, as with the good ole' boy, this does not necessarily mean the rapid closer is bad for the development of a solution that can best address your need. Just be prepared for a fast ride!

## Never Ending Talker

Without my even defining the never ending talker, I suspect you are thinking, "I have seen this sales executive in my office!" This sales executive loves to discuss your need ad nauseam, think out loud the potential solutions, and then pontificate well beyond reason in every meeting you have. One of the business development executives I used to work with referred to this approach as "show up and throw up." The sales executive shows up and basically throws up on the customer spewing all kinds of information and solutions.

As a sales leader, I have had a few never ending talkers who reported to me. And, while they can be productive – most drive me and our customers to the brink. This includes lost deals just because the customers cannot endure another long-winded session.

One such sales executive who reported to me was working on an international BPO program for a well-known global financial services company. I am not sure the customer ever really had a compelling reason to do business with us, but the sales executive kept at it. He would meet with the customer, present different solutions and, well, just talk! I participated in a couple of these sessions – and even I decided I could not endure much more. The developed solution was intriguing, but not enough to waste the time of any of us involved in the opportunity – not the least of which was the customer. To make matters worse, this was not a large revenue opportunity for us, and did not include much potential profit. Yet, the never ending talker continued on, and on.

After twelve months (yes, an entire year), I finally had the conversation with him that he had to either close the deal or let it go. It took another couple of months, but he finally advised the customer that we were going to end the opportunity as "lost." If down the road the customer believed there was any value, we could certainly reopen it. But, for now, the deal was dead.

Although I don't know for certain, I imagined the customer was dancing on his desk at the possibility that the never ending talker would actually stop calling him!

So, this begs the question … is there any value in a never ending talker? Well, the short answer is, "Yes." As odd as it seems, the never ending talker has the ability to dissect a need and offer up a potential array of solutions. For I have found that as much orating as a talker provides – they generate just as much thought into solving a need. In fact, some of the most creative solutions I have seen have come from the never ending talker. It is possible, however, that this is more the exception than the norm.

## Empathizer

The empathizer is the sales executive who takes pride in placing himself in the shoes of the customer to gain a feel for the pain being experienced by the need or current state. Many believe this is one of the most important characteristics in being an effective sales representative or sales executive. While I think it is important to be able to empathize with a customer, I find this approach can come across as patronizing, phony, and at times even a bit silly. In addition, the empathizer often fails to get the necessary support from their own company.

If I were to put myself in the position of a strategic sourcing executive, I would be more focused on seeking subject matter expertise and the ability to address the need rather than empathy alone. That said, it's worth noting that when married up with other selling personas, empathizing with a sourcing executive or team and the identified need can be a valuable trait.

Early in my sales management career, I hired an empathizer. In fact, this was his primary approach to closing deals. Once he had an appointment, he immediately turned his attention to making the customer feel as if he completely understood how frustrating and dire the need was. But, there was rarely any substance to this approach. And, at the end of his first year he had a number of customers where he had great relationships – but no closed deals.

I suspicioned it was because he had spent so much time empathizing with his customers that he failed to really solve their needs. He got the message, and took his empathy approach to a level where he married it up with increased subject matter expertise and a focus on solving for the need. As a result, he began solving needs for customers through sold solutions and became an excellent producer in the organization.

## Creative Thinker

The creative thinker is the individual who can evaluate a need for a customer, and develop out-of-the-box solutions. This sales executive is akin to a "think tank" professional. Often they will develop solutions that no one else has thought of ... including those in the same company. This is where "cutting edge" comes from. The benefit to having creative thinkers involved is they cause both the customer and provider to think about approaching the solution differently. This may result in a solution that is completely different than anyone expects. And, while the results from this approach may be a wild and expensive alternative, I have seen many situations where the creative thinker develops solutions that are highly affordable – if not big cost savers over the current state and other potential solution offers.

Candidly, I enjoy working with the creative thinkers ... probably because I have always wanted to be more of one than I am. And, I love hanging around folks who can take a situation and off the cuff start brainstorming great potential solutions that no one else has ever thought of.

There is a potential downside. Sometimes the creative thinker can get so caught up in the development of a creative and ideal solution, that they lose focus on solving the need within a reasonable amount of time. Or, the cost to implement the creative idea may far exceed any rational budget. But, that alone does not mean this sales executive should be dismissed.

## Strategist

The strategist is the sales executive who looks for the most strategic solution to solve a particular need. This is the person who will look at solving the problem in the most expeditious manner, while developing an effective ROI and ensuring the solution aligns with the goals and culture of your organization. Often this individual is juggling a few balls in the air to ensure the solution hits all of these criteria.

The strategist will usually be a subject matter expert, or has the ability to bring SMEs on board to help with the solution. In addition, they will demonstrate a strong ability to understand the culture of your organization so that once a solution is proposed both you and the potential provider know it will work. And, finally, the strategist will be cognizant of the financial impact of the solution. This means a full understanding of the costs your company will incur to buy the solution, and the return on investment it will provide – both near-term and years down the road.

---

If you are like me, you may be thinking that a hybrid of a couple or more of the above sales executive personality types would be ideal. There are positives from each; but, two rise to the top for me. While I consider myself a strategist who has the ability to recruit creative thinkers to work with me on specific opportunities, combining these two personas might just be the perfect sales executive.

Regardless of the personality types, a solid professional relationship between the sourcing executive and sales executive can be the difference between selecting a marginal solution and an ideal one. This does not mean the two have to be best friends. But, a mutual and working business relationship that allows for interactive discussion and openness between the parties is essential.

I often wonder when these relationships don't exist, or are strained, if the most ideal solution is passed up in favor of lesser alternatives. Since buying and selling, particularly at strategic levels, is a people business this relationship is extremely important.

# Key Points

- The relationship between the sourcing executive and sales executive can heavily influence the outcome of the go-forward solution.  Buying and selling is a people business.
- Sourcing Executive personas
  - Pushover
  - Strategic thinker
  - VIP
  - Hard ass
- Sales Executive personas
  - Good ole' boy
  - Rapid closer
  - Never ending talker
  - Empathizer
  - Creative thinker
  - Strategist

# 11
# EACH OF US HAS A JOB TO DO

In the business world each of us has a job to do – whether it is in the role of a sourcing executive or that of a sales executive. For as long as I have been working I have heard the phrase, "Nothing in business happens until someone *sells* something." While this may be true, I might also suggest that nothing in business happens until someone *buys* something. While the intent of these phrases is not to make light of other necessary aspects of running a business, buying and selling are critical components for companies to succeed. I have heard so many sourcing executives state they would never want to be in the role of a sales executive. But, the truth is sales executives have the same feeling about sourcing executives. The reality is both are challenging jobs – in their own respective ways. And, it takes the right individuals to accomplish both.

In reviewing the steps on the path beginning with an identified need through implementing the optimal solution, there is a surprising alignment among the sourcing executive / team and the sales executive. Each milestone in the process has an aligned goal between both parties. This includes defining the need, identifying potential providers, requesting proposals for potential solutions, understanding the financial model, selecting the go-forward partner, and the contracting phase that leads up to the program launch.

As you think about each of these milestones, you can begin to see the alignment.

## Figure 11.1 – Pathway to Finding the Optimal Solution

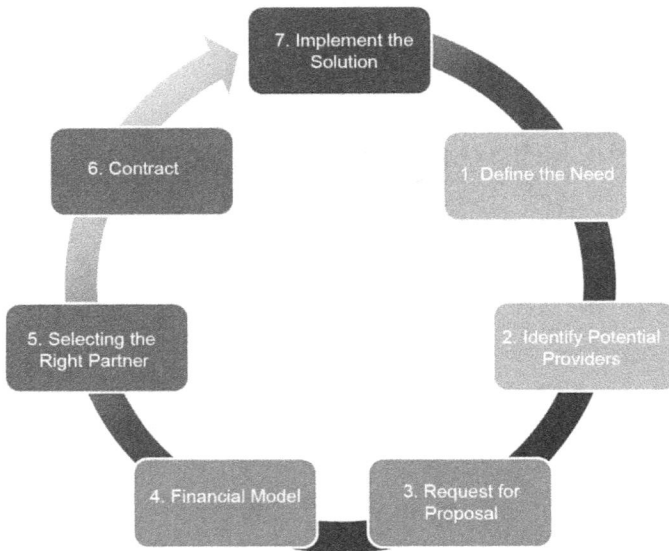

1. **Define the Need** – While you want to ensure the need is appropriately identified, the provider community also wants to know they are building a solution that fully meets the need as you see it. Include them in the process to help you define the need such that all parties are on the same page. This may mean going back to the need after you identify the group of potential providers.

2. **Identify Potential Providers** – Both sides of the table want to know the potential providers are right for the need. No one wants to waste time building a solution where the provider(s) may not be able to solidly address the need.

3. **Request for Proposal** – As a sourcing executive you want to ensure the information received in a proposal provides a solution that will address your need. And, the sales executive wants to ensure the proposal they deliver does exactly the same thing.

4. **Financial Model** – Top of mind for every sourcing executive *and* sales executive is:

   a. *Can the provider make money with the proposed solution?* It's obvious why the provider wants to make money on a proposed solution. But, as a sourcing executive you also want to ensure the provider turns a profit. This is what will keep them in business, and ensure they can continue delivering the solution to you.

   b. *Is there a financial business case to support the proposed solution?* If the financial business case is not inviting, both parties lose out on solving the need.

      While working to build a solution for the need, this is where it makes sense for the potential providers and the sourcing team to work closely to determine if a financial business case can be developed.

5. **Selecting the Right Partner** – Not being selected as the go-forward partner will often bring disappointment. But, selecting the right partner is beneficial to the provider community and your company. No one wants to enter into a business relationship by selecting the wrong partner.

6. **Contract** – While this is a legal document aimed at addressing the "what ifs" in a business relationship, it clearly signifies an intent to work together.

7. **Implement the Solution** – This is where the rubber meets the road. As a sales executive, I clearly know sourcing teams put their necks on the line each time they select a go-forward partner. Ensuring success at this point is a defining milestone. It means the same to the sales executive who has spent as much time as you getting to this point.

# It's Not Always about a Specific Need

While I have outlined a very methodical process to buying solutions that solve needs in organizations, it may be in the best interest of both parties to engage in dialog outside of any specific situation. Waiting until a sourcing initiative presents itself may add undue pressure whereas engaging in conversations when there is no immediate need allows for a much more comfortable, if not thorough process.

With one of the largest clients I worked, we had a number of contracts running concurrently. However, both the customer and our company were constantly looking for additional opportunities to expand our relationship. The customer, an international banking and financial services company, recognized that the more business they could provide us, the better their overall financial model would be. At the same time, we believed we could leverage our staff and existing customer relationships to more rapidly execute on newly installed programs – assuming we could address the specific needs.

The problem was the customer didn't have a full grasp of other services we could offer. And, we didn't have visibility into strategic initiatives that were on the bank's horizon. So, we proposed an offsite meeting at an executive retreat in upstate New York that would include the executives of both organizations and their respective teams. The idea was to hold this meeting at a location where there would be almost no interruptions from either of our companies. From the bank, the executive vice president of strategic sourcing led the initiative. And, the head of sales from our company was the executive sponsor.

To start the session, the bank laid out all of their strategic initiatives for the coming year. This included some that were already in play – and where progress had been made. But, it also included those where an identified solution had not yet been determined. In some cases, how to get the initiative off the ground had not even been discussed. They truly shared their entire strategic plan for the coming year. The plan was so comprehensive, that it took the executive vice president of strategic sourcing half of the first day to get through the content. While there was some discussion throughout his presentation, most of the time was spent describing the initiatives and laying out the strategy.

At the end of that session, our company responded with the various initiatives we were pursuing – specifically what our coming year would look like from a strategic perspective.

With each individual plan laid out, the following day was spent white-boarding where we believed we could match up our services to the bank's initiatives. It was a brainstorming session – with a good bit of creative input from both sides. At the end of the second day, we had a roughly sketched game plan to address several of the bank's sourcing initiatives. Granted, there were a lot of homework and follow-up assignments as a result of the session – but we knew, at a high level, where the potential opportunities were.

The session allowed both of our companies to learn more about each other in an open forum. And, the identified opportunities addressed needs neither of us had thought about prior to the meeting. The fact that we both approached the session in advance of any formal sourcing initiative allowed for a more comfortable meeting with a great deal of interactive discussion, focused on actually solving open needs of the bank.

While this type of approach will not be practical in every sourcing / sales relationship, the mutual benefits may far exceed any conceivable expectations.

---

A well-managed process to addressing and sourcing needs as they arise in your organization will ultimately lead to best-in-class solutions and partners. Ultimately these sourcing decisions can affect your entire company. But, know that the same thing can be said for the partner you choose to help solve your need. Each party should view the relationship as a partnership that drives their respective businesses forward. When you have accomplished this, you have achieved a true sourcing executive / sales executive relationship versus a buyer / sales representative.

# Key Points

- Nothing in business happens until someone sells or buys something!
- There is a methodical seven-step process to fulfilling a need with an optimal solution:
  1. Define the need
  2. Identify potential providers
  3. Request for proposal
  4. Financial model
  5. Selecting the right partner
  6. Contract
  7. Implementation.
- A well-managed process to addressing and sourcing needs as they arise in your organization will ultimately lead to best-in-class solutions and partners.

# GLOSSARY OF TERMS

**Budget and Expense Statement (B&E)** – a financial statement that compares actual expenses to a planned budget over a specified period of time.

**Business Process Outsource (BPO)** – transitioning a current internally managed / run operation to a partner outside of the company.

**Buyer** – an individual who sources a specific product, often a commodity, looking for the best price in the market.

**Cost Benefit Analysis (CBA)** – a financial deep dive into determining if a solution and identified partner will provide the desired financial payback or cost benefit if implemented. It is represented by the formula Current State Costs – Recommended Solution = Cost Benefit.

**Electronic Bidding Tool** – a web-based tool used by buyers to source a need that allows sellers to make specific entries and commitments in a consistent manner.

**Executive Dashboard** – a one-page document used to keep executive leadership aware of the overall status of an implementation. It should contain four quadrants: key milestone deliverables, critical accomplishments, key risks and issues, and the next 30 days.

**Financial Business Case** – an assessment of a need and potential solutions to determine if pursuing an optimal solution is viable for the business. There are two levels of a financial business case: initial business case and cost benefit analysis.

**Gantt Chart** – a project management tracking tool with rows and columns that identifies specific tasks to be accomplished in an implementation. Most contain identified resources, targeted completion dates and dependencies.

**Gap Analysis** – a table that identifies specific elements of a current state, recommended go-forward solution, the risk (or gap), and the required mitigation.

**Guard Rail** – a certain parameter agreed upon by both parties that provides some guidance on what can and cannot be included in a solution, program or contract.

**Initial Business Case** – a high-level determination of whether you should invest in pursuing a solution and engaging potential partners.

**Key Milestones** – a roll-up of major deliverable categories in an implementation. This is derived from the detail in a project plan and provides a quick glance as to how the project is progressing, at a high level without having to sift through the drill-down detail of an entire project plan.

**Master Services Agreement (MSA) / Contract / Agreement** – legal document between two parties that formally governs the terms and conditions of a business relationship.

**Non-Disclosure Agreement (NDA)** – legal document intended to protect sensitive data that may be shared between two parties during a business relationship.

**Request for Information (RFI)** – process used to identify a group of potential providers that may be able to help a company solve for a need.

**Request for Proposal (RFP)** – process used to identify a specific solution and partner(s) that will solve a specific need.

**Return on Investment (ROI)** – a financial performance measure used to evaluate the benefit of investing in a strategic solution for an identified need.

**Reverse Auction** – type of auction where sellers bid for the prices at which they are willing to sell their goods and services to buyers.

**Sales Executive** – highly skilled individual that works to understand the customer's business requirements and match those up with solutions their company can offer.

**Sales Representative** – individual who sells commodity products or mature solutions. These products and solutions often have very little strategic value.

**Soft Dollars** – elements of a current state or recommended solution that add residual value – such as workflow improvement, increased efficiency, or ease of doing business; but, stop short of offering any financial impact to the solution.

**Sourcing Curve** – evolution of a sourcing need from a newly identified requirement in the marketplace to a solution that has become mature and commoditized over time.

**Statement of Work (SOW)** – document subordinate to, and often a schedule of the MSA that addresses the business requirements of a specific program.

**Strategic Sourcing Executive** – individual who looks to solve a problem where a need has arisen that often has not previously been sourced or fully defined; a re-engineering need of an existing solution has emerged; or the company is looking to optimize a solution that works, but is not in its ideal state.

**Term Sheet** – a document in advance of an MSA that identifies the business issues to be addressed in a formal MSA. This document often becomes the basis of negotiating a formal agreement.

**Total Cost of Ownership** – a strategic approach of understanding all of the costs of a specific business operation, well beyond the unit cost to buy a product.

**Trusted Partner** – a current business partner and provider with your company where you have a successful business relationship.

**Unit Cost** – the cost of a specific product, exclusive of the costs to use or implement the product in the business operation.

# ABOUT THE AUTHOR

Todd A. Leonard is a managing partner in the consulting firm Alleon Group. Prior to that, he was vice president of business development for Taylor Communications, Inc.

While he has spent most of his career in sales or sales management, he also led the implementation services organization at Standard Register. While there, he helped define and build a professional services consulting firm to address business / marketing communications and sourcing. Prior to his role in business development he was managing director of the financial services business unit, where he led the marketing and sales efforts across the company.

Todd has worked with a variety of companies in the financial services, transportation, manufacturing, professional services and healthcare markets. He also has extensive experience in working with consulting firms – specifically in the strategic sourcing space.

When not selling, Todd, who is an Eagle Scout, plays an active role in the Boy Scouts of America. He serves on national event staffs and as a volunteer scouter in his local community. A member of Mandarin Presbyterian Church, Todd lives in Jacksonville FL, is married and has two children.

www.ingramcontent.com/pod-product-compliance
Lightning Source LLC
Chambersburg PA
CBHW060559210326
41519CB00014B/3518